Social Media

Social Media

Principles and Applications

Pavica Sheldon

LEXINGTON BOOKS
Lanham • Boulder • New York • London

Published by Lexington Books
An imprint of The Rowman & Littlefield Publishing Group, Inc.
4501 Forbes Boulevard, Suite 200, Lanham, Maryland 20706
www.rowman.com

Unit A, Whitacre Mews, 26-34 Stannary Street, London SE11 4AB

British Library Cataloguing in Publication Information Available

Library of Congress Cataloging-in-Publication Data

Sheldon, Pavica, 1980-
Social media : principles and applications / Pavica Sheldon.
pages cm
Includes bibliographical references and index.
ISBN 978-0-7391-9264-1 (cloth : alk. paper) -- ISBN 978-0-7391-9265-8 (electronic)
1. Online social networks. 2. Social media. 3. Interpersonal communication. I. Title.
HM742.S54 2015
302.23'1--dc23
2015011602

∞ ™ The paper used in this publication meets the minimum requirements of American
National Standard for Information Sciences Permanence of Paper for Printed Library
Materials, ANSI/NISO Z39.48-1992.

Printed in the United States of America

This book is dedicated to my husband, Luke, who not only supported me in the process of writing this book, but also encouraged me to write it. He has provided support and love when I needed it the most.

Contents

Introduction

This book examines principles and applications of social media in interpersonal, mass-mediated, educational, organizational, and political settings. Social media technologies take on many different forms, including social network sites like Facebook and Twitter, blogs, wikis, online video and photo-sharing sites (e.g., Pinterest), rating and social bookmarking sites, and video/text chatting sites (e.g., Skype). The first three chapters of the book focus on the principles of social media. The first chapter explores how interpersonal communication theories could be applied to our understanding of social media. The theories explained in this chapter are uncertainty reduction, social penetration, social exchange, expectancy violations, and communication privacy management theory. The second chapter explores how mass communication theories could be applied to our understanding of social media. Theories examined in this chapter include uses and gratifications, agenda-setting, framing, cultivation, and spiral of silence theory. The third and last chapter in section I focuses on personality psychology and individual differences of people who use social media. The chapter provides an overview of media psychology research as it relates to users and nonusers of social media. It explores personality traits that are theoretically linked to online self-presentation, including narcissism, extroversion, self-efficacy, the need to belong, and the need for popularity. When it comes to social media, researchers have particularly focused on narcissism and extroversion, as these directly relate to social media use. Other personality constructs studied in relation to social media include shyness, loneliness, and sensation seeking.

Section II contains six chapters covering applications of social media in a variety of settings. Chapter 4 explains the application of social media in politics, mentioning both political campaigns in the United States and political movements around the world that have been facilitated by the use of Twitter and Facebook. The fifth chapter explains the changing definition of privacy due to the role technology plays in our life. The sixth chapter explores the benefits and challenges of using social media in education. It reports the results of experimental studies supporting the use of blogs, YouTube, and Twitter in the college classroom. It further explains the dynamics of the student-teacher relationship on Facebook. Chapter 7 details the role of social media in disaster communication. Chapter 8 outlines the pros and cons of advertising on social media sites, and further provides guidelines for how to advertise on Facebook, Twitter, YouTube, Pinterest, and LinkedIn. The last chapter, chapter 9, focuses on social media addiction. It discusses problems with defining social media addiction, its causes and consequences. Although many newspaper articles have focused on the negative aspects of social media, very few research studies have been conducted in this area.

Overall, this book answers some of the following questions: Who uses social media? Can we develop meaningful relationships through social media? How do people use social media during natural disasters and crises? How do people use social media to get social support and evoke political change? Is privacy dead? How do employers use social media to check on employees? How do teachers and students communicate using social media? How do advertisers use social media to promote their products and services? Why are people addicted to social media?

I

Principles of Social Media

ONE

Social Media and Traditional Interpersonal Communication Theories

This chapter explores the application of interpersonal communication theories to the understanding of social media, primarily social network sites and blogs. The theories explained in this chapter are uncertainty reduction, social penetration, social exchange, expectancy violations, and communication privacy management theory.

UNCERTAINTY REDUCTION THEORY

Uncertainty reduction theory was introduced in 1975 by Berger and Calabrese in order to predict and explain relational development between strangers. The theory posits that interpersonal relationships develop as individuals reduce uncertainty about each other (Berger, 1979; Berger & Calabrese, 1975). Most people find the state of uncertainty uncomfortable and try to increase the predictability of the behaviors (behavioral uncertainty) and attitudes and beliefs (cognitive uncertainty) of other individuals. If individuals are unable to "get to know" each other, the possibility that they will develop an enduring relationship is reduced (Berger & Calabrese, 1975).

To reduce interpersonal uncertainty, individuals engage in various information-seeking strategies (Berger, Gardner, Parks, Schulman, & Miller, 1976): (1) passive strategies through which the information seeker collects information about a target person by observing his or her behavior; (2) active strategies that involve proactive efforts to gain knowledge about another person, usually by asking a third party about the target person; and (3) interactive strategies that require direct communication with a target of information seeking. Interpersonal communication, in one or another form, is the primary means of uncertainty reduction. As uncertainty levels decline, information-seeking behavior decreases (Axiom 3).

Individuals' strategies to decrease uncertainties in face-to-face interaction can be applied in computer-mediated settings such as social network sites (SNSs) as well. For example, Antheunis, Valkenburg, and Peter (2010) examined which uncertainty reduction strategies (passive, active, interactive) the members of social network sites used to gain information about persons whom they have recently met. They discovered that the passive uncertainty reduction strategy was most commonly employed among the users of Hyves, a Dutch site similar to Facebook; however, the interactive strategy was the only strategy that effectively reduced the level of uncertainty. Other researchers (Parks & Floyd, 1996; Ramirez, Walther, Burgoon, & Sunnafrank, 2002; Tidwell & Walther, 2002) have also argued that in dyadic computer-mediated communication (CMC), participants mostly employed interactive strategies.

Users of social network sites can employ a variety of other tactics to reduce uncertainty. They can, for example, observe another person unobtrusively via his or her personal profile (Walther, Van Der Heide, Kim, Westerman, & Tong, 2008), or ask a third person about the user that they have just added as a Facebook "friend." While we often cannot see our Facebook friends in person, we can observe their behavior by focusing on their status messages and the photographs that they choose to post, as well as the biographic information posted on their profiles (Sheldon & Pecchioni, 2014).

One of the interactive strategies for uncertainty reduction used evocatively by the information seeker is self-disclosure (Berger et al., 1976). *Self-disclosure* refers to intentional sharing of information about oneself, including personal experiences, ideas and attitudes, feelings and values, and even dreams, hopes, ambitions, and goals. Wheeless and Grotz (1976, p. 47) define self-disclosure as "any message about the self that a person communicates to another." Unlike other forms of CMC, social network sites usually encourage users to disclose a great deal of information about themselves (Antheunis et al., 2010), including private information such as hobbies, tastes in music, books, movies, relationship statuses, and sexual preferences (Gross & Acquisti, 2005).

Jourard (1971) explained the tendency to disclose in established relationships as the "dyadic effect"—the more information one receives, the greater his or her willingness to self-disclose. Several studies (e.g., Craig & Wright, 2012; Sheldon, 2013) have found that greater depth and breadth of self-disclosure to a Facebook friend leads to greater predictability of that friend's behavior. In other words, the more friends talk to each other, the less uncertainty they experience. This supports Axiom 1 of uncertainty reduction theory. Axiom 1 states that as the amount of verbal communication between strangers increases, the level of uncertainty for each interactant (about the other in the relationship) decreases (West & Turner, 2010). Later, Berger (1987) updated his theory, arguing that the process of uncertainty reduction is relevant in developed relationships as well as initial interactions. While, historically, uncertainty reduction theory has been developed to explain traditional face-to-face interactions, recent studies show that it can help explain the development of SNS relationships.

SELF-DISCLOSURE AND SOCIAL ATTRACTION

Early studies of relationship development (e.g., Worthy, Gary, & Kahn, 1969) have reported that self-disclosure is rewarding to a recipient, and people will give more rewards to those whom they like. In other words, people tend to disclose intimate information to persons they like and withhold intimate information from persons whom they do not like (Axiom 7 of uncertainty reduction theory, Berger & Calabrese, 1975). This has been true for face-to-face relationships (e.g., Certner, 1973; Fitzgerald, 1963; Worthy et al., 1969) as well as computer-mediated communication (Collins & Miller, 1994; Levine, 2000; Park, Lee, & Kim, 2006; Ramirez, Walther, Burgoon, & Sunnafrank, 2002). Sheldon (2013) discusses how Facebook friends who have just added each other disclose to each other more if they have previously been socially attracted to each other. These findings are also in line with Theorem 5 of uncertainty reduction theory (Berger & Calabrese, 1975) which suggests that people tend to disclose intimate information to persons they like and withhold intimate information from persons whom they do not like. Additionally, self-disclosure might provoke social attraction in return (Sheldon & Pecchioni, 2014). We tell our stories to people that we like, but we also tend to like those to whom we self-disclose. As Jourard (1959) suggested a half century ago, the act of self-disclosure is personally rewarding and cathartic, and such positive feelings lead to liking.

Sheldon and Pecchioni (2014) found that the process of relationship maintenance, in terms of the relationships among social attraction, self-disclosure, and predictability, is relatively similar in both exclusively Facebook and exclusively face-to-face relationships. Their findings indicated a positive and significant relationship between social attraction and self-disclosure between two exclusive Facebook friends. They also found a positive and significant relationship between self-disclosure and predictability in exclusive Facebook relationships. Regardless of the medium through which participants interact, self-disclosure is significantly related to the prediction of that friend's behavior.

SELF-DISCLOSURE AND TRUST

Another factor that influences how much uncertainty exists in a relationship is trust.

Although there is a great variability among individuals in the extent to which they trust others, trust is critical in understanding when we choose to share personal information with others and when we choose secrecy (Joinson, Reips, Buchanan, & Paine-Schofield, 2011; Kerr, Stattin, & Trost, 1999; Wheeless & Grotz, 1977). High levels of trust are markers of close interpersonal relationships (Anderson & Emmers-Sommer, 2006; Bukowski & Sippola, 1996; Rempel, Holmes, & Zanna, 1985). Trust is critical to reducing uncertainty face to face (Dainton & Aylor, 2001), and this seems to work as well with social network sites. In a study examining the best Facebook friendships, Sheldon (2009) found that the more certain we are about another person's behavior, the more we trust him or her. Sheldon and Pecchioni (2014) found that the more trust we have in our exclusive Facebook friends and our exclusive face-to-face friends, the more we self-disclose to them. The more we trust them, the more we can predict their behavior. These findings are in line with earlier face-to-face studies (Foubert & Sholley, 1996; Steel, 1991) suggesting that of all personality factors, trust is the most influential in predicting self-disclosure. However, when comparing the amount of trust between two pairs of friends, the Sheldon and Pecchioni (2014) study showed that respondents trust their Facebook friends less than their face-to-face friends. Bane, Cornish, Erspamer, and Kampman (2010) examined female bloggers' perceptions of online and "real-life" same-sex friendships, and they found that participants perceive trust, loyalty, emotional support, and practical help as more likely to occur in a real-life friendship than in an online friendship. These findings support previous studies (Parks & Roberts, 1998) showing that online relationships are lower in interdependence, understanding, and commitment than real-life relationships.

SOCIAL PENETRATION THEORY

Another theory that can help explain the role of self-disclosure in the development of relationships is *social penetration theory*. Altman and Taylor (1973) conceptualized social penetration theory to illustrate the process of relationship bonding (social penetration) that moves a relationship from superficial to more intimate. Intimacy is defined as physical, intellectual, and emotional, while the social penetration process includes both verbal and nonverbal behaviors. Most relationships follow some particular trajectory, or pathway to closeness. According to the theory, relationship development is a gradual process, systematic and predictable, while self-disclosure is at its core. Altman and Taylor used the metaphor of an onion to explain self-disclosure. Disclosure begins on the outer layer and proceeds to the core of the onion. The outer layer of a person is what is available to others. It is comprised of superficial information about ourselves (e.g., preferences in music, clothing, food, etc.) that we share with other people early in the relationship. The sufficiently motivated information-seeker will try to penetrate every layer until he reaches the very core of another person's self. The inner core of the onion is information typically known by only a few people and includes strong feelings, values, beliefs, and self-concept (Altman & Taylor, 1973).

The penetration can be viewed along two dimensions: breadth and depth. *Breadth* refers to the number of various topics discussed in the relationship. *Depth* refers to the degree of intimacy that guides topic discussions. Information at the depth level is more significant and more central to our self-identity. Altman and Taylor (1987) argued that as relationships move toward intimacy, a wider range of topics is discussed (breadth), with several of the topics to be intimately discussed (depth).

Although some studies have suggested that people disclose significantly more in their Internet relationships than face to face (Parks & Floyd, 1996), recent studies (Tang & Wang, 2012; Sheldon & Pecchioni, 2014) have challenged those ideas. Tang and Wang (2012) surveyed 1,027 Taiwanese bloggers, exploring the topics that the bloggers disclosed on their blogs, as well as the depth and breadth of what the bloggers self-disclosed to three target audiences (online audience, best friend, and parents). Tang and Wang discovered that bloggers made the deepest and widest disclosures of their thoughts, feelings, and experiences to their best friends in the real world—rather than to their parents or online audiences. Bloggers seemed to be aware of the risks of self-disclosure online, and therefore avoided disclosing personal and financial matters. Sheldon and Pecchioni (2014) also indicated that college students self-disclose less to their Facebook friends than to their face-to-face friends. However, social attraction is the most important predictor of the number and variety of topics (breadth) that individuals discuss among each other on Facebook and face to face—while the intimacy level is the most important predictor of the depth of their discussions (depth dimension of self-disclosure) (Sheldon & Pecchioni, 2014). This supports the "onion model"—as we get to know somebody more, we tend to disclose more intimate topics to him or her. It is clear then why social attraction only has an influence on how many different topics we choose to discuss with one another. Other studies (Krasnova, Spiekermann, Koroleva, & Hildebrand, 2010) have argued that the depth of self-disclosure is not relevant to social network sites. Depth of self-disclosure is "a highly subjective variable" as "the economic value of a platform is not defined by how intimate users' revelations are, but rather by their participation and interaction" (Krasnova et al., 2010, p. 113).

Jin (2013) analyzed multiple layers of private disclosure on the micro-blogging site Twitter. The results show that there are five different components of private disclosure: (1) daily lives and entertainment; (2) social identity; (3) competence; (4) socio-economic status; and (5) health. Information related to daily lives and entertainment was located in the outermost layer of the social penetration onion, being the type of information that users reveal more frequently (the breadth dimension of private disclosure). Health-related private information was located in the innermost layer of the onion, meaning that users are reluctant to share it publicly (depth dimension).

If it happens, self-disclosing through social media can have a positive impact. Olson (2012) conducted a study using both a survey and a focus group that asked participants how good they feel when they disclose on Facebook. Eighty-one percent of the survey participants agreed that they feel good when they self-disclose on Facebook, and most focus group participants agreed that self-disclosing on Facebook had a positive effect on one's self-esteem. They argued that most people post positive events on Facebook and therefore feel very good about themselves. Bronstein (2013) summarized research on blogging, showing that personal blogs are becoming increasingly popular places where people disclose personal information to complete strangers—often feeling less fearful of potential condemnation or ridicule. The reason is not the personal anonymity, as most bloggers prefer to publish their real names, but a social anonymity—"the physical invisibility that characterizes online communications and gives bloggers the power over the content on their blogs and over the identity they choose to reveal or conceal from their audience" (Bronstein, 2013, p. 173). Bronstein (2012) writes about bloggers being able to release emotional stress by venting feelings, thoughts, and ideas in an online environment less threatening than face-to-face communication. McKenzie (2008) and Ko and Chen (2009) also report that through self-disclosure bloggers experience positive feelings, such as satisfaction and excitement, which significantly influence their perception of subjective well-being.

Social penetration theory is grounded in several of the principles of social exchange theory.

SOCIAL EXCHANGE THEORY

In 1959, Thibaut and Kelley wrote that "every individual voluntarily enters and stays in any relationship only as long as it is adequately satisfactory in terms of his or her rewards and costs" (p. 37). Thibaut and Kelley's originally-named theory of interdependence—now known as *social exchange theory*—argues that people evaluate their relationships in terms of costs and rewards. *Costs* are those elements in the relationship that have a negative value to a person (e.g., stress, time, energy, attention).

Rewards are those elements in the relationship that have a positive value to a person (e.g., fun, loyalty, attention) (as cited in West & Turner, 2010). Sabatelli and Shehan (1993) use the metaphor of a marketplace to explain how relationships function. According to social exchange theory (SET) the worth of a relationship predicts its outcome. Positive relationships are those whose worth is positive (i.e., rewards exceed costs). Negative relationships are those whose worth is negative (i.e., costs exceed rewards). Positive relationships are continued. Negative relationships will likely be terminated (West & Turner, 2010).

The first assumption of social exchange theory is that relationships are interdependent. The outcome for a relationship is never in the hands of only one individual. Partners co-create the outcome. Whenever one member of a relationship acts, both the other member and the relationship as a whole are influenced. The second assumption of the theory is that relational life is a process. Time affects exchanges because past experiences in a relationship are often used to guide judgments and expectations about rewards and costs. The standards that humans use to evaluate costs and rewards vary over time and from person to person. What is viewed as a reward by one person may be seen as a cost by another, and vice versa (West & Turner, 2010).

Another standard for evaluating a relationship, according to Thibaut and Kelley (1959), includes two types of comparisons: comparison level and a comparison level for alternatives. A comparison level (CL) refers to a standard representing what people feel they should receive in the way of rewards and costs from a particular relationship. A comparison level for alternatives (CLalt) refers to the minimum level of relational rewards that an individual is willing to accept (Roloff, 1981). A person typically measures this minimum level of what he or she is willing to accept based on the rewards that are available from alternative relationships—as well as from rewards that are available from remaining alone. Some researchers argue (e.g., Walker, 1984) that CLalt offers a good way to explain why some women stay in abusive relationships.

Several studies have applied social exchange theory to the phenomenon of social networking. Drussell (2012) argued that the amount of time and energy one designates to texting or posting comments and status updates on Facebook relates directly to perceived rewards—including the number of "likes" or responses. Posting a Facebook or Twitter update requires a little time and effort, but the potential rewards are unrestricted—especially if a person has a large audience. Drussell (2012) discusses the concept of power as it relates to social exchange theory. Power is the control over the rewards and punishments. Some people have social power and therefore the ability to influence the behavior and thoughts of others. In other words, the more friends a person has on social networks, the greater the amount of perceived status and power the person has. This power might be reflected in the rejection of friend requests from another person.

Krasnova et al. (2010) also used social exchange theory to learn what motivates users to disclose personal information on Facebook and StudiVZ, a popular German online social network. Their focus group results showed that the convenience of relationship maintenance was the most important factor leading users to share information through the online social network platform. This motive was closely followed by the enjoyment and the desire to build new relationships. Other studies have identified relationship maintenance as the main motive for Facebook use (e.g., Sheldon, 2008). On the cost side, Krasnova et al. found that perceived privacy risks were the main factors discouraging users from disclosing information on SNSs. Participants mentioned that they would engage in a conscious "privacy calculus" when deciding whether or not to self-disclose. According to SET, humans evaluate their relationships in terms of costs and rewards.

Users in the Krasnova et al. (2010) study admit that they are aware of the risks when disclosing information on social network sites, but they do so to gain certain benefits. Those benefits include efficiently communicating with a large group of friends at the same time by posting one status, as well as possibilities for reciprocation. Other benefits include relationship building—disclosing more about themselves in order to build new friendships.

EXPECTANCY VIOLATIONS THEORY

Another theory that was developed to explain face-to-face interactions but can also explain online relationships is *expectancy violations theory* (Burgoon, 1978). According to the theory, human interaction is driven by expectations. Three factors influence expectations: individual communicator factors (gender, personality, age, appearance), relational factors (prior relational history, status differences, levels of attraction and liking), and context factors (formality/informality, social/task function, environmental restrictions, cultural norms) (Burgoon & Hale, 1988).

Expectations for human behavior are learned. People learn their expectations from the culture in which they were born. For example, the expectations about a student-teacher relationship in the United States are that teachers are knowledgeable about the subject matter and available to students who need help. When expectations are violated, the violation is judged as either positive or negative, depending on the reward potential of others. West and Turner (2010) provide an example of the expectancy violations: a prolonged stare from a person on public transportation is perceived less favorably than a stare from a romantic partner.

Originally, the concept of "expectancy violations" was developed to explain nonverbal violations of behavioral norms. Later it was used to explain both verbal and nonverbal expectancies. Recently, the theory has been used to explain behavior on social network sites. McLaughlin and Vitak (2012), for example, explored how norms on social network sites evolve over time and how violations of these norms impact an individual's self-presentational and relationship goals. They hypothesized that Facebook norms might be different from traditional offline norms, as Facebook friendships include a wide range of connections, including those of close friends, college classmates, family members, and acquaintances. Facebook norms are also expressed implicitly, meaning that they are not written down but are understood by the group in general (Burnett & Bonnici, 2003). In McLaughlin and Vitak's (2012) study, focus group participants indicated that they had learned how to conduct themselves on Facebook by observing how other users behaved. Thus, users would post more if they saw friends doing so. Almost all participants agreed that it was rude to ignore a friend request from someone they had met in person. That is the expected norm. There are also expectations about the use of the "wall" and the use of private messages. Participants indicated that they expect to use the wall and status updates to share videos, jokes, birthday wishes, etc., while they use private messages and chat to give out personal information, organize an event, or start a discussion thread for a small group. The most frequently reported norm violation on Facebook was too many status updates. The next most reported violation was overly emotional updates, including relationship fights and other public feuds. McLaughlin and Vitak (2012) report that the most frequent reaction to a negative expectancy violation was to delete the "friend" on Facebook or "hide" their status updates in news feeds.

Student-teacher relationships on Facebook are another area where violations of expectations might happen. Several studies have warned faculty to be careful when adding students as Facebook friends. Both Karl and Peluchette (2011) and Schwartz (2009) have argued for faculty being open to new technology but also taking a passive stance by not initiating friendships with students themselves, but only responding to their requests. As Karl and Peluchette (2011) found, some students still get irritated by requests from their professors. In a Malesky and Peters (2012) study, nearly 40 percent of students and 30 percent of faculty believed that it is inappropriate for professors to even have an account on social network sites. Students viewed the professors' actions as being more appropriate only when they are trying to assist their students (e.g., learn their names or offer extra credit).

In 2013, Sheldon surveyed faculty members to learn what their expectations for friending students are. Almost 50 percent of surveyed faculty members said that they are currently a Facebook friend with one or more students. This number was much higher than the number reported in a

2010 study of faculty members' friendships with students at Ohio colleges of pharmacy (Metzger, Finley, Ulbrich, & McAuley, 2010). This might suggest that the attitudes toward informal student-teacher relationships are changing. More faculty members are recognizing the benefits of having students as Facebook friends. As attitudes change, the norms change (Sheldon, 2014). Some of the norms reflect with whom the users share private information.

COMMUNICATION PRIVACY MANAGEMENT THEORY

According to *communication privacy management theory* (Petronio, 2002), people make choices and rules about what to tell others, and what to withhold from others, based on a "mental calculus" grounded in criteria such as culture, gender, and context (as cited in West & Turner, 2010). Petronio uses the term "private disclosure" rather than "self-disclosure." Private disclosure refers to the process of communicating private information to another. The theory further argues that there is a line between being public and being private (private boundaries). When people reveal private information to others, the boundary around the shared information is called a collective boundary.

People make a decision to reveal or conceal private information depending on five criteria: culture, gender, motivations, context, and risk-benefit ratio. For example, different cultures have different norms for privacy and openness. Men and women seem to be socialized to develop different rules for how privacy and disclosure operate. People may be motivated to disclose private information in order to develop close relationships. Certain environments invite disclosures, while others caution against them. Finally, the rules are based on risk-benefit criteria, which is similar to the bases for rules in social exchange theory. People evaluate the risks relative to the benefits of disclosing (as cited in West & Turner, 2010).

According to the control and ownership supposition of communication privacy management theory, people feel that they own private information about themselves and are in control of to whom else they grant access. When access to private information is closed, boundaries are thick; when access is open, people have thin boundaries in place. Boundary turbulence includes conflicts about boundary expectations and regulation. Turbulence may surface when the co-owners of information do not explicitly negotiate how they want to share their private information with third parties (Petronio, Jones, & Morr, 2003). Communication privacy management is a dialectic theory, which means that people have needs for both protection (for autonomy) and access (for social interaction). Petronio (2002) argues that these two forces are in constant interplay with one another and that privacy tensions cannot be understood as a dualism.

Recently, the theory has been used to explain the "privacy paradox," or why users disclose personal information on social network sites while at the same time expressing concern about privacy. According to boyd (2010), "a conversation you might have in the hallway is private by default, public through effort," but on the Facebook wall "the conversation is public by default, private through effort." In other words, information shared face to face is something people easily forget, whereas information shared online is stored and archived and is easily replicated. Jin (2013) discusses the difference between protected tweets (thick walls; Petronio, 2002) and public tweets (thin walls; Petronio, 2002). Tweets that Twitter users post on their own wall are self-generated content, while the tweets other users post are other-generated content. Jin's survey of Twitter users, nonusers, and dropouts revealed that nonusers have concerns about privacy and are reluctant to sign up for a Twitter account.

Teachers deal with privacy dialectics on a daily basis when they try to decide what information they want to reveal to their students and what they want to conceal. Most studies (e.g., Sorensen, 1989; Andersen, Norton, & Nussbaum, 1981), however, report a positive relationship between teacher self-disclosures and the student perception of affective learning. A teacher's verbal behaviors, including the use of personal examples, create a more immediate classroom environment—which is also positively related to affective and cognitive learning (Christensen & Menzel, 1998; Gorham, 1988). Mazer, Murphy, and Simonds (2007) found that when a female teacher discloses certain information, such as with personal pictures and opinions on certain topics, students perceive similarities between themselves and the instructor. A majority of college student participants perceived a teacher's use of Facebook positively although they warned professors to be "themselves" on Facebook so they can "get a better feel for their personality."

Child, Petronio, Agyeman-Budu, and Westermann (2011) applied CPM theory to explore the process of privacy rule adaptations for blogging by examining situations that have triggered bloggers to delete or modify a post ("blog scrubbing"). Their survey of 356 personal journal-type bloggers revealed that bloggers actually stop to review what they write. They are driven by risk assessment and motivations to scrub posted content. This desire to remove information is explained as the bloggers' high concern for accurately portraying themselves through blog content. Moreover, Madden and Smith (2010) report that 47 percent of young adult users engage in blog scrubbing through deleting comments and posts. They thus apply a post hoc privacy management decision criteria (Petronio, 2002).

Metzger and Pure (2009) studied to what extent Facebook users alternatively erect thin, moderate, or thick boundaries around their personal profile information in terms of (1) the privacy settings they implement; (2) how much information they disclose in their profile; and (3) their "friending" behavior. Overall, the findings showed that Facebook users prefer a thin to moderate boundary to balance their competing desires for privacy and publicity. Users said that they are more likely to disclose information that could help them maintain or enhance social relationships, but would less likely disclose information that could negatively impact relationship formation or personal safety. Most participants were very liberal in their friending behavior, befriending people that they have never met in person. In terms of gender differences, studies indicate (Metzger & Pure, 2009; Tufekci, 2008) that females desire greater control over personal information posted online, and while less likely to disclose contact information, they are more likely to post photos of themselves and others.

Gibbs and Cho (2010) first examined cultural differences in privacy management among social media users. They studied American Facebook users and Korean Cyworld users. While Facebook users were more likely to control privacy settings related to the visibility of their profiles, Cyworld users were more likely to control searchability. Facebook users also had more friends than Cyworld users, but their relationships were less intimate. Gibbs and Cho's (2010) findings might be explained by individualistic versus collectivistic cultural values. Koreans have thick boundaries for out-group members, but thin boundaries with in-group members. Previous studies (e.g., Triandis, 1989) also showed that collectivistic cultures strictly differentiate between in-groups and out-groups; in other words, members of collectivistic cultures do not use SNS networks for social capital, but rather for maintaining a close circle of friends with whom they have fewer privacy concerns (Gibbs & Cho, 2010). Ellison, Steinfield, and Lampe (2007) previously found that the main benefit of Facebook among American students is the advantage of weak ties.

Communication privacy management theory has been utilized to examine how young adult Facebook users respond to their parental Facebook friend requests. Child and Westermann's (2013) study of 235 individuals found that most young adults accept Facebook friend requests from both mothers and fathers. Most participants did not make any restrictive privacy rule adjustments in regard to the requests. However, young adults who accepted requests from their mothers without restrictive privacy adjustments came from families that value openness and transparency. Such individuals also had a higher overall level of relational quality with their mothers. Closeness and trust were not important factors in accepting Facebook requests from fathers. Child and Westermann (2013) explained those findings by reference to the roles each parent plays in a family. Mothers are socialized to be caregivers, and experience closer relationships with children than fathers do. In late adolescence, progeny experience the father's role as discliplinarian (McKinney & Renk, 2008).

Overall, most research about self-disclosure in interpersonal face-to-face environments stresses the benefits of disclosure for building new relationships; however, most research about disclosure online emphasizes the risks of disclosure (Metzger & Pure, 2009).

SUMMARY

This chapter contrasts how social media impacts upon computer-mediated communication versus face-to-face communication. Five theories are presented that examine and explain relational development: uncertainty reduction theory, social penetration theory, social exchange theory, expectancy violation theory, and communication privacy management theory. Each of the theories examines what it is that either directly or indirectly progresses participants from unfamiliarity to bonding.

An overarching observation is that the two contexts are essentially similar, with common strategies and tactics employed to form relationships, yet some differences remain. One study applying uncertainty reduction theory, as an example, found that although trust is a key element in predicting self-disclosure both online and offline, respondents actually trusted their Facebook friends less than their face-to-face friends. Another unique element examined in this chapter is the "privacy paradox," which relates solely to the disclosure of personal information on social network sites. An underpinning of this paradox is that while users continue to disclose personal information online, they are still more wary of repercussions of the disclosure. This paradox does not exist in face-to-face communications as information is not archived and stored for later reference.

REFERENCES

Altman, I., & Taylor, D. (1973). *Social penetration: The development of interpersonal relationships*. New York: Holt, Rinehart, Winstron.

Altman, I., & Taylor, D. (1987). Communication in interpersonal relationships: Social penetration processes. In M. Roloff & G. Miller (Eds.), *Interpersonal processes* (pp. 257-277). London, England: Sage Publications.

Andersen, J. F., Norton, R. W., & Nussbaum, J. F. (1981). Three investigations exploring relationships between perceived teacher communication behaviors and student learning. *Communication Education, 30*, 377-392. doi:10.1080/03634528109378493.

Anderson, T. A., & Emmers-Sommer, T. M. (2006). Predictors of relationship satisfaction in online romantic relationships. *Communication Studies, 57*, 153-172. doi:10.1080/10510970600666834.

Antheunis, M. L., Valkenburg, P. M., & Peter, J. (2010). Getting acquainted through social network sites: Testing a model of online uncertainty reduction and social attraction. *Computers in Human Behavior, 26*, 100-109. doi:10.1016/j.chb.2009.07.005.

Bane, C., Cornish, M., Erspamer, N., & Kampman, L. (2010). Self-disclosure through weblogs and perceptions of online and "real-life" friendships among female bloggers. *CyberPsychology, Behavior & Social Networking, 13,* 131-139. doi:10.1089 /cyber.2009.0174.

Berger, C. R. (1979). Beyond initial interaction: Uncertainty, understanding, and the development of interpersonal relationships. In H. Giles & R. St. Clair (Eds*.), Language and social psychology* (pp. 122–144). Oxford: Basil Blackwell. doi:10.1111/j.1468-2958.1975.tb00258.x.

Berger, C. R. (1987). Communicating under uncertainty. In M. E. Roloff & G. R. Miller (Eds.), *Interpersonal processes* (pp. 39-62). Newbury Park, CA: Sage.

Berger, C. R., & Calabrese, R. J. (1975). Some explorations in initial interaction and beyond: Toward a developmental theory of interpersonal communication. *Human Communication Research, 1,* 99-112. doi: 10.1111/j.1468-2958.1975.tb00258.x.

Berger, C. R., Gardner, R. R., Parks, M. R., Schulman, L. S., & Miller, G. R. (1976). Interpersonal epistemology and interpersonal communication. In G. R. Miller (Ed.), *Explorations in interpersonal communication* (pp. 149-172). Newbury Park, CA: Sage Publications.

boyd, d. m. (2010). Making sense of privacy and publicity. SXSW. Austin, Texas.

Bronstein, J. (2012). Blogging motivations for Latin American blogosphere: A uses and gratifications approach. In T. Dumova & E. Fiordo (Eds.), *Blogging in the global society: Cultural, political and geographical aspects* (pp. 200-215). Hershey, PA: Information Science Reference. doi:10.4018/978-1-60960-744-9.ch012.

Bronstein, J. (2013). Personal blogs as online presences on the internet: Exploring self-presentation and self-disclosure in blogging. *Aslib Proceedings, 65,* 161-181. doi:10 .1108/00012531311313989.

Bukowski, W. M., & Sippola, L. K. (1996). Friendship and morality: (How) are they related? In W. M. Bukowski, A. F. Newcomb, & W. W. Hartup (Eds.), *The company they keep* (pp. 238-261). Cambridge, MA: Cambridge University Press.

Burgoon, J. (1978). A communication model of personal space violations: Explication and an initial test. *Human Communication Research, 4,* 129–142. doi:10.1111/j.1468-2958.1978.tb00603.x.

Burgoon, J. K., & Hale, J. L. (1988). Nonverbal expectancy violations: Model elaboration and application to immediacy behaviors. *Communication Monographs, 55,* 58-79. doi:10.1080/03637758809376158.

Burnett, G., & Bonnici, L. (2003). Beyond the FAQ: Explicit and implicit norms in Usenet news-groups. *Library and Information Science Research, 25,* 333–351. doi:10.1016/S0740-8188(03)00033-1.

Certner, B. C. (1973). Exchange of self-disclosures in same-sexed groups of strangers. *Journal of Consulting and Clinical Psychology, 40,* 292–297. doi:10.1037/h0034446.

Child, J. T., Petronio, S., Agyeman-Budu, E. A., & Westermann, D. A. (2011). Blog scrubbing: Exploring triggers that change privacy rules. *Computers in Human Behavior, 27,* 2017-2027. doi:10.1016/j.chb.2011.05.009.

Child, J. T., & Westerman, D. A. (2013). Let's be Facebook friends: Exploring parental Facebook friend requests from a communication privacy management (CPM) perspective. *Journal of Family Communication, 13,* 46-59. doi:10.1080 /15267431.2012.742089.

Christensen, L. J., & Menzel, K. E. (1998). The linear relationship between student reports of teacher immediacy behaviors and perceptions of state motivation, and of cognitive, affective, and behavioral learning. *Communication Education, 47,* 82-90. doi:10.1080/03634529809379112.

Collins, N. L., & Miller, L. C. (1994). Self-disclosure and liking: A meta-analytic review. *Psychological Bulletin, 116,* 457-475. doi:10.1037/0033-2909.116.3.457.

Craig, E., & Wright, K. B. (2012). Computer-mediated relational development and maintenance on Facebook. *Communication Research Reports, 29,* 119-129. doi:10.1080 /08824096.2012.667777.

Dainton, M., & Aylor, B. (2001). A relational uncertainty analysis of jealousy, trust, and maintenance in long-distance versus geographically close relationships. *Communication Quarterly, 49,* 172-188. doi:10.1080/01463370109385624.

Drussell, J. (2012). *Social networking and interpersonal communication and conflict resolution skills among college freshmen.* Master of Social Work Clinical Research Paper, 21. Retrieved from http://sophia.stkate.edu/msw_papers/21.

Ellison, N., Steinfield, C., & Lampe, C. (2007). The benefit of Facebook "friends:" Social capital and college students' use of online social network sites. *Journal of Computer-Mediated Communication, 12*(4), article 1. doi:10.1111/j.1083-6101.2007.00367.x.

Fitzgerald, M. P. (1963). Self-disclosure and expressed self-esteem, social distance, and areas of the self revealed. *The Journal of Psychology, 56,* 405–412. doi:10.1080/00223980.1963.9916655.

Foubert, J., & Sholley, B. K. (1996). Effects of gender, gender role, and individualized trust on self-disclosure. *Journal of Social Behavior and Personality, 11,* 277-288.

Gibbs, J. & Cho, S. E. (2010). *A cross-cultural investigation of privacy management in Facebook and Cyworld.* Presented at the International Communication Association conference.

Gorham, J. (1988). The relationship between verbal teacher immediacy behaviors and student learning. *Communication Education, 37,* 40-53. doi:10.1080/03634528809378702.

Gross, R., & Acquisti, A. (2005). Information revelation and privacy in online social networks (The Facebook case). In *ACM workshop on privacy in the electronic society* (pp. 71-80). Alexandria: USA. doi:10.1145/1102199.1102214.

Jin, S. A. (2013). Peeling back the multiple layers of Twitter's private disclosure onion: The roles of virtual identity discrepancy and personality traits in communication privacy management on Twitter. *New Media & Society, 15,* 813-833. doi:10.1177/1461444812471814.

Joinson, A. N., Reips, U. D., Buchanan, T. B., & Paine-Schofield, C. B. (2011). Privacy, trust, and self-disclosure online. *Human-Computer Interaction, 25,* 1-24. doi:10.1080/07370020903586662.

Jourard, S. M. (1959). Self-disclosure and other-cathexis. *Journal of Abnormal and Social Psychology, 59,* 428-431. doi:10.1037/h0041640.

Jourard, S. M. (1971). *Self-disclosure: An experimental analysis of the transparent self.* New York: Robert E. Krieger.

Karl, K. A., & Peluchette, J. V. (2011). "Friending" professors, parents and bosses: A Facebook connection conundrum. *Journal of Education for Business, 86,* 214-222. doi:10.1080/08832323.2010.507638.

Kerr, M., Stattin, H., & Trost, K. (1999). To know you is to trust you: Parents' trust is rooted in child disclosure of information. *Journal of Adolescence, 22,* 737–752. doi:10.1006/jado.1999.0266.

Ko, H., & Chen, T. (2009). *Understanding the continuous self-disclosure of bloggers from the cost-benefit perspective.* Proceedings of the 2nd Conference on Human System Interactions. Cantania, Italy. doi:10.1109/HSI.2009.5091033.

Krasnova, H., Spiekermann, S., Koroleva, K., & Hildebrand, T. (2010). Online social networks: Why we disclose. *Journal of Information Technology, 25,* 109-125. doi:10.1057/jit.2010.6.

Levine, D. (2000). Virtual attraction: what rocks your boat. *Cyber Psychology & Behavior, 3,* 565-573. doi:10.1089/109493100420179.

Madden, M., & Smith, A. (2010). *Reputation management and social media: How people monitor their identity and search for others online.* Pew Internet and American Life Project website. Retrieved from http://www.pewinternet.org/Reports/2010/Reputation-Management.aspx

Malesky, L. A., & Peters, C. (2012). Defining appropriate professional behavior for faculty and university students on online social networking websites. *Higher Education, 63,* 135-151. doi:10.1007/s10734-011-9451-x.

Mazer, J. P., Murphy, R. E., & Simonds, C. J. (2007). I'll see you on "Facebook": The effects of computer-mediated teacher self-disclosure on student motivation, affective learning, and classroom climate. *Communication Education, 56,* 1-17. doi:10.1080/03634520601009710.

McKenzie, H. M. (2008). *Why bother blogging? Motivations for adults in the United States to maintain a personal journal blog.* Unpublished master's thesis. North Carolina State University, Raleigh, NC.

McKinney, C., & Renk, K. (2008). Differential parenting between mothers and fathers: Implications for late adolescents. *Journal of Family Issues, 29,* 806-827. doi:10.1177 /0192513X07311222.

McLaughlin, C., & Vitak, J. (2012). Norm evolution and violation on Facebook. *New Media and Society, 14,* 299-315. doi:10.1177/1461444811412712.

Metzger, A. H., Finley, K. N., Ulbrich, T. R., & McAuley, J. W. (2010). Pharmacy faculty members' perspectives on the student/faculty relationship in online social networks. *American Journal of Pharmaceutical Education, 74*(10), 188.

Metzger, M., & Pure, R. (2009). *Privacy management in Facebook.* Presented at the annual meeting of National Communication Association.

Olson, A. M. (2012). *Facebook and social penetration theory.* Master's thesis. Gonzaga University.

Park, J. Y., Lee, J. E., & Kim, N. (2006). *"Hi! My name is Clora": The effects of self-disclosing agents on the attitude and behavior of users.* Presented at the annual meeting of the International Communication Association, Dresden, Germany.

Parks, M. R., & Floyd, K. (1996). Making friends in cyberspace. *Journal of Communication, 46,* 1-17. doi:10.1111/j.1460-2466.1996.tb01462.x.

Parks, M. R., & Roberts, L. D. (1998). Making MOOsic: The development of personal relationships on line and a comparison to their off-line counterparts. *Journal of Social and Personal Relationships, 15,* 517-537. doi:10.1177/0265407598154005.

Petronio, S. (2002). *Boundaries of privacy: Dialectics of disclosure.* New York: State University of New York Press.

Petronio, S., Jones, S., & Morr, M. C. (2003). Family privacy dilemmas: Managing communication boundaries within family groups. In L. R. Frey (Ed.), *Group communication in context: Studies of bona fide groups* (pp. 23–55). Mahwah, NJ: Erlbaum.

Ramirez, A., Jr., Walther, J. B., Burgoon, J. K., & Sunnafrank, M. (2002). Information seeking strategies, uncertainty, and computer-mediated communication: Toward a conceptual model. *Human Communication Research, 28,* 213-228. doi:10.1111/j.1468-2958.2002.tb00804.x.

Rempel, J. K., Holmes, J. G., & Zanna, M. P. (1985). Trust in close relationships. *Journal of Personality and Social Psychology, 49,* 95-112. doi:10.1037/0022-3514.49.1.95.

Roloff, M. E. (1981). *Interpersonal communication: The social exchange approach.* Beverly Hills, CA: Sage.

Sabatelli, R. M., & Shehan, C. L. (1993). Exchange and resource theories. In P. G. Boss, W. J. Doherty, R. LaRossa, W. R. Schumm, & S. K. Steinmetz (Eds.), *Sourcebook of family theories and methods: A contextual approach* (pp. 385-411). New York: Plenum. doi:10.1007/978-0-387-85764-0_16.

Schwartz, H. L. (2009). Facebook: The new classroom commons? *Chronicle of Higher Education, 56*(6), B12–13.

Sheldon, P. (2008). The relationship between unwillingness to communicate and students' Facebook use. *Journal of Media Psychology, 20,* 67-75. doi:10.1027/1864-1105.20.2.6.

Sheldon, P. (2009). I'll poke you. You'll poke me! Self-disclosure, social attraction, predictability and trust as important predictors of Facebook relationships. *Cyberpsychology: Journal of Psychosocial Research on Cyberspace, 3,* article 1.

Sheldon, P. (2013). Examining gender differences in self-disclosure on Facebook versus face-to-face. *The Journal of Social Media in Society, 2,* 89-106.

Sheldon, P. (2014). *Examining student-teacher relationship on Facebook: Theory of reasoned action and uses and gratifications.* Paper presented at the annual meeting of the Association for Education in Journalism and Mass Communication (AEJMC), Montreal, Canada.

Sheldon, P., & Pecchioni, L. (2014). Comparing relationships between self-disclosure, liking and trust in exclusive Facebook and exclusive face-to-face relationships. *American Communication Journal, 16*(2).

Sorensen, G. (1989). The relationship among teachers' self-disclosive statements, students' perceptions, and affective learning. *Communication Education, 38,* 259-276. doi:10.1080/03634528909378762.

Steel, J. L. (1991). Interpersonal correlates of trust and self-disclosure. *Psychological Reports, 68,* 1319-1320. doi:10.2466/pr0.1991.68.3c.1319.

Tang, J., & Wang, C. (2012). Self-disclosure among bloggers: Re-examination of social penetration theory. *Cyberpsychology, Behavior, and Social Networking, 15,* 245-250. doi:10.1089/cyber.2011.0403.

Thibaut, J., & Kelley, H. (1959). *The social psychology of groups.* New York: Wiley.

Tidwell, L. C., & Walther, J. B. (2002). Computer-mediated effects on disclosure, impressions, and interpersonal evaluations: Getting to know one another a bit at a time. *Human Communication Research, 28,* 317-348. doi:10.1111/j.1468-2958.2002.tb00811.x.

Triandis, H. C. (1989). The self and social behavior in different cultural contexts. *Psychological Review, 3,* 506-520. doi:10.1037/0033-295X.96.3.506.

Tufekci, Z. (2008). Can you see me now? Audience and disclosure regulation in online social network sites. *Bulletin of Science, Technology and Society, 28,* 20–36. doi:10.1177/0270467607311484.

Walker, L. (1984). *The battered woman syndrome.* New York: Springer.

Walther, J., Van Der Heide, B., Kim, S., Westerman, D., & Tong, S. T. (2008). The role of friends' appearance and behavior on evaluations of individuals on Facebook: Are we known by the company we keep? *Human Communication Research, 34,* 28-49. doi:10.1111/j.1468-2958.2007.00312.x.

West, R., & Turner, L. H. (2010). *Introducing communication theory: Analysis and application* (4th ed). Boston: McGraw-Hill Higher Education.

Wheeless , L. R., & Grotz , J. (1976). Conceptualization and measurement of reported self-disclosure. *Human Communication Research, 2,* 338-346. doi:10.1111/j.1468-2958.1976.tb00494.x.

Wheeless, L. R., and Grotz, J. (1977). The measurement of trust and its relationship to self-disclosure. *Human Communication Research, 3,* 250-257. doi:10.1111/j.1468-2958.1977.tb00523.x.

Worthy, M., Gary, A. L., & Kahn, G. M. (1969). Self-disclosure as an exchange process. *Journal of Personality and Social Psychology, 13,* 59–63. doi:10.1037/h0027990.

TWO

Social Media and Theories of Mass Communication

This chapter examines how traditional mass communication theories that were developed to explain the uses and effects of newspaper, radio, and television are used and applied in our understanding of social media. Theories examined in this chapter include uses and gratifications, agenda-setting, framing, cultivation, and spiral of silence.

USES AND GRATIFICATIONS THEORY

Uses and gratifications theory (U&G; Katz, Blumler, & Gurevitch, 1973) has been used in a number of studies to understand why people use particular media. Unlike other media theories (e.g., cultivation theory), the theory does not focus on the content of the media. It emphasized the user and their active role in choosing media that can satisfy one or more of their needs. Katz, Blumler, and Gurevitch (1973) emphasize that we choose a specific medium that can fulfill our need gratification. Those needs could be classified into four categories: diversion (escape from daily problems), personal relationships (using media for companionship), personal identity (reinforcing values), and surveillance (information that helps an individual accomplish something) (McQuail, Blumler, & Brown, 1972). For example, we watch comedy shows when we want to laugh, and we watch CNN when we want to be informed. According to the theory, people are self-aware, and they are able to explain why they use the media.

Uses and gratifications is a heuristic theory, which means that it has stimulated a lot of research of both traditional and new media (Internet and social media). In the last ten years a number of studies have examined uses and gratifications for Facebook use (Krause, North, & Heritage, 2014; Sheldon, 2008; Smock, Ellison, Lampe, & Wohn 2011), Twitter (Chen, 2011; Johnson & Yang, 2009), YouTube (Hanson & Haridakis, 2008), Pinterest (Mull & Lee, 2014), Yelp (Hicks et al., 2012), and blogs (Kaye, 2005; 2010). This has resulted in new gratifications being added to explain how individuals use social media. For example, virtual community is a "new" gratification added to explain communications with people met through the Internet (Song, LaRose, Eastin, & Lin, 2004). Social media have changed the importance of some gratifications. For example, while most people watch television to get information or gratify entertainment needs, most people use social network sites to maintain relationships (Sheldon, 2008). Some social network sites (e.g., LinkedIn) satisfy professional advancement needs, while others allow individuals expressive information sharing (as cited in Smock et al., 2011). Krause, North, and Heritage (2014) studied motivations for using music-listening applications on Facebook. They found a new gratification that they called the habitual diversion gratification. This motive is not commonly seen among reasons for using other Facebook features. Mull and Lee (2014) examined the user gratifications obtained from Pinterest, an image-sharing social networking site. A confirmatory factor analysis revealed five dimensions of uses and gratifications obtained from the image-sharing SNS: fashion, creative projects, entertainment, virtual exploration, and organization. Creative projects and organization motivations were not identified in previous U&G studies pertaining to social network sites.

Research suggests that the patterns and motives behind social media usage are, in part, a function of demographic and personality variables. However, studying how social and personal characteristics influence our Facebook use (in general) is not enough, because different types of people might use different features (Smock, Ellison, Lampe, & Wohn, 2011). As Smock et al. argue: "Facebook is more usefully conceived of as a collection of tools utilized in different ways to meet different needs" (p. 2323). In their study, only three motivations (relaxing entertainment, expressive information sharing, and social interaction) were predictive of general use, but six other motivations predict the use of specific features. For example, expressive information sharing was a predictor of the use of status updates and groups, but not one-to-one communications (private chats). Thus, those who want to share how their day went will not do it through a private message to a friend; instead, they will post it publicly so that everyone can see it. The social interaction motive significantly predicted the use of messages, chat, and wall posts. Professional advancement predicted the use of wall posts and private messages.

Fewer studies (Chen, 2011; Johnson & Yang, 2009) have investigated the motives for Twitter use. The main reasons for Twitter use are social and information motives (Johnson & Yang, 2009). Social motives include having fun, to be entertained, relax, see what others are up to, pass the time, express oneself freely, keep in touch with friends or family, communicate more easily, and communicate with many people at the same time. Information motives include to get information, give or receive advice, learn interesting things, meet new people, and share information with others. Johnson and Yang (2009) found that users were primarily motivated to use Twitter for its informational aspects, arguing that the reason is the capacity of Twitter to easily customize which stream of content to consume. Twitter users can follow certain users and news organizations and are thus able to avoid the information overload that other Internet news sites bring.

YouTube is another social media site that was examined from the audience-centered perspective. Hanson and Haridakis (2008) found different motives for watching and sharing different types of news-related content. Viewers of news in a more traditional format were doing so primarily for information reasons; viewers of news in comedy and satire formats were doing so primarily for entertainment. Interpersonal communication motives predicted the sharing of news videos on YouTube. In a later study, Haridakis and Hanson (2009) examined individual differences (social activity, interpersonal interaction, locus of control, sensation seeking, innovativeness, and YouTube affinity) predicting viewing and sharing videos on YouTube. While users viewed videos for information seeking, they viewed and shared videos for entertainment, co-viewing, and social interaction. Internal locus of control predicted the sharing of YouTube videos. It is then obvious that internally controlled users have more self-confidence and that people use sites such as YouTube to enhance their social circles and social lives (Haridakis & Hanson, 2009). Interpersonal interaction, sensation seeking, innovativeness, and YouTube affinity were not related to viewing or sharing YouTube videos. This communicates something about the purpose of YouTube as a video-sharing and social network site. Unlike Facebook, where users go to interact with their friends interpersonally (through private messages and chat), YouTube is a place where users go for entertainment and social interaction. This is illustrated through a number of viral videos that get shared from one user to another through other social network sites.

The reasons for producing YouTube videos, however, are different than the reasons for viewing or sharing them. Producers like to express themselves. Mosemghvdlishvili and Jansz (2013) studied the motivations of YouTubers who create videos about Islam. They conducted interviews with producers of videos on Islam. The analysis revealed three dominant motivational factors: communicating Islam, self-expression, and social recognition. The communicating Islam factor was the primary motivation among the Muslim producers who said that they use videoblogging to remove the misconceptions that people have regarding Islam. In terms of self-expression, all respondents agreed that they like YouTube, because it allows them to express themselves more openly, while allowing experimentation with appearance and style.

Not many studies have focused on the rating sites. Hicks et al. (2012) explored motivations for using the crowd-sourcing and social network site Yelp. The site functions as a rating system mostly for restaurants and smaller businesses. Yelp also sells ads and sponsors listings for small businesses. Hicks et al. (2012) found that the main reason people use it is information sharing, followed by entertainment, and convenience. This is somewhat different from the relationship maintenance and entertainment motives for using Facebook and YouTube. Other types of rating services, such as ratemyprofessor.com (RMP) or koofers.com, have not received much research interest. One study (Kowai-Bell, Guadango, Little, Preiss, & Hensley, 2011) examined the effect that RMP content has on the expectations and approaches to the reviewed classes. It would be interesting to find out why students utilize those sites, either as the posters or the readers.

Another form of social media that has received significant attention from the U&G theorists are blogs. Although blogs are not as popular as SNSs anymore, they still exist. While the first blogs were political, more popular blogs today are personal blogs in the form of a journal, or news blogs in the form of an online news aggregator (e.g., Huffington Post). The first study (Kaye, 2005) examining motivations for blog use found that the main reasons were political and social surveillance, followed by convenience, and then personal fulfillment. Kaye (2010) also developed a uses and gratifications measurement scale for blogs, citing the following motives: convenient information seeking, anti-traditional media sentiment, expression/affiliation, guidance/opinion seeking, blog ambiance, personal fulfillment, political debate, variety of opinion, and specific inquiry. One of the more recent studies on how young users use blogs was conducted by Armstrong and McAdams (2011). They found that individuals who use blogs for information-seeking purposes are more likely to trust the content in the blogs than those who use blogs for leisure activities. Again, there is a difference between the readers of blogs and the producers of blogs. Nardi, Schiano, Gumbrecht, and Swartz (2004) identified five motivations that bloggers report as the reasons for writing their blogs. Those included: to document one's life, to provide commentary and opinions, to use as a form of catharsis through expressing deeply held emotions, finding one's own thoughts through writing, and to be part of a community.

AGENDA-SETTING THEORY

According to *agenda-setting theory* (McCombs & Shaw, 1972), media are not always successful at telling us what to think, but they are quite successful at telling us what to think about. According to the theory, what is covered in the news becomes what people say is important to them. In other words, the "media agenda" determines the "public agenda." While hundreds of studies have focused on how television news shapes public opinion, most research studying social media from the agenda-setting perspective has focused on testing reverse agenda-setting and intermedia agenda-setting.

While the traditional model explaining the five factors that contribute to the media agenda (individual journalists, media routines, organizational factors, social institutions, and cultural/ideological considerations; Shoemaker & Reese, 2014) does not include social media, we know that in many cases it is the citizen journalists who are the source, and often the breaker of, the news. The notion of reverse agenda-setting, where journalists respond to public interests and thus public agenda precedes and influence media agenda, has been a topic of study over the last several years. Kim and Lee (2007) introduced the idea of reversed agenda-setting where public agenda sets the media agenda. On social media, the public is represented by anyone with an account. Goode (2009) defined them as "citizen journalists." Citizen journalism represents practices where ordinary users engage in journalistic activities, such as blogging about the current events, photo and video sharing, and posting eyewitness commentary (Goode, 2009, p. 1288). Citizen journalists played important roles in the uprisings of the Arab Spring in 2010 (see chapter 4), during the Iranian revolution in 2009, and in the 2014 Ferguson unrests. The Ferguson unrests include protests that occurred after the fatal shooting of Michael Brown on August 9, 2014, in Ferguson, Missouri. Brown died after being shot by a Ferguson police officer.

Russell Neuman, Guggenheim, Mo Jang, and Bae (2014) studied how social media might contribute to the reversed agenda-setting. Although Russell Neuman et al. (2014) suspected that social media agenda most likely will not set the traditional media agenda, they found that the social media do not slavishly follow the traditional news media agenda. For example, online blogs discuss social issues such as birth control, abortion, and same-sex marriage more than the traditional media, while traditional media focus more on issues of economics.

Grzywinska and Borden's (2014) study focused on the impact of social media on agenda building and agenda-setting in traditional media by examining the case study of the Occupy Wall Street movement. The Occupy Wall Street movement started on July 13, 2011 as an idea inspired by events that occurred in the "Arab Spring" (see chapter 4). Protesters defined themselves as "the 99 percent of lower wage earners who do not agree with greed and corruption of the 1 percent top wage earners" (Grzywinska & Borden, 2014, p. 2). Just like protesters in Egypt and Tunisia in 2010, the Occupy Wall Street protesters used social media to announce their next gatherings, to sign up for a newsletter, or to discuss issues with other activists (Grzywinska & Borden, 2014). In 2011, the authors investigated the relationship of newspapers' coverage (the *New York Times*, the *Washington Post*, the *Los Angeles Times*) of the Occupy Wall Street events, with the activities on the two largest Facebook pages dedicated to the movement. Their results showed that traditional media used other traditional media as a source of reference more often than social media—which used it rarely. Social media was more frequently cited by other social media channels. Grzywinska and Borden (2014) concluded that there is a tendency for media channels to keep users "within the fold"; however, social media sometime set the agenda for traditional media and influence their coverage. As the authors argued, traditional journalists did not have other sources of information about the movement other than social media. The process through which the media choose which events, issues, or sources to feature over others is called agenda building (McCombs, 2004).

Volders (2013) studied agenda-setting theory in the political discourse on Twitter. This was the first study to focus on agenda-setting on Twitter. Volders's results revealed that Twitter activity regarding politics is mainly due to traditional media coverage. Traditional media refer to newspapers, magazines, radio, and television. One example, however, revealed strong reversed agenda-setting effects where a collection of Twitter messages became so prominent that traditional media placed it on their agenda. Few studies have examined agenda-setting and reversed agenda-setting when it comes to social media. The most developed area of research on the influence of social media on agenda-setting is the one that examines the role of blogs. Several studies have found that blogs have actually contributed to the redistribution of power between traditional media and citizen media (Drezner & Farrell, 2004; Meraz, 2009).

There are more studies to support that social media and traditional media influence each other's agenda. This influence of mass media agendas on each other is called intermedia agenda-setting (Lopez-Escobar, Llamas, McCombs, & Lennon, 1998). Several studies (Groshek & Groshek Clough, 2013; Ragas & Kiousis, 2010; Sayre, Bode, Shah, Wilcox, & Shah, 2010) have suggested that SNSs can be important intermedia agenda-setting agents due to their capacity to quickly and easily share stories and break news. Kwak, Lee, Park, and Moon (2010) compared CNN Headline News and trending topics on Twitter, and found episodes of news breaking first on Twitter. In a study of the 2009 Morgan Harrington missing-person case, Artwick (2012) found that the agenda on Twitter was set by a combination of blogs, entertainment, and other types of non-news websites. Groshek and Groshek Clough (2013) have used a time-series analysis to track intermedia agenda setting across two leading traditional media outlets (the *New York Times* and CNN), as well as the most trending topics on two popular SNSs (Facebook and Twitter). Their results revealed that the potential for SNSs to directly shape media agendas does exist but only on certain topics. Thus, Twitter was more likely to follow political agendas formed by traditional media, and cultural coverage on Facebook was more clearly set by agendas on traditional media. However, cultural coverage on Twitter was the one category of coverage where a social media channel set the agenda for a traditional one. Groshek and Groshek Clough (2013) suggested studying media agendas not only from a topical perspective but also temporally. Messner and Distaso (2008) content-analyzed 2,059 articles over a six-year period from the *New York Times* and the *Washington Post* and found that the newspapers increasingly legitimized blogs as credible sources (30–40 percent of articles cited a blog as a source). Blogs have also heavily relied on traditional media as sources. Messner and Distaso (2008) concluded that the traditional media and blogs contribute to a news source cycle, in which news content can be passed back and forth from one media to the other.

FRAMING THEORY

Framing theory focuses on the way the content of a message is delivered by media and interpreted by receivers (Chung & Cho, 2013; Iyengar, 1991). Different categorizations of frames exist. According to one group of researchers (e.g., Semetko & Valkenburg, 2000), there are two types of frames: generic and issue-specific. Generic frames deal with broader themes, while issue-specific frames are more detailed. Generic frames include broad themes such as conflict, economic, or human interest stories. Issue-specific frames provide in-depth issue-specific information (Wasike, 2013). Another researcher (Iyengar, 1991) distinguishes between episodic and thematic frames. Episodic frames focus on events and stories, while thematic frames focus on trends over time, emphasizing the context and environment. While episodic frames focus on an individual, thematic frames focus on an issue. Yet another group of researchers (Borah, 2014; Cappella & Jamieson, 1997) differentiates between strategy and value frames in political communication. Strategy frames use the language of wars and competition (Cappella & Jamieson, 1997), while value frames resonate with individuals' preexisting schema and reinforce existing values.

Framing theory has been very popular among the scholars examining political communication. The theory is important because media define what political issues or aspects are important; frames therefore influence public opinion. The political arena is saturated with individuals who try to frame issues in their favor (Bichard, 2006). Recently, politicians have taken advantage of social media by using them to communicate with the public directly through framing. The first use of framing analysis concerning social media started with blogs (e.g., Bichard, 2006; Guillory, 2007). For example, Bichard (2006) investigated frames used on candidate websites in the 2004 presidential election. They analyzed four framing attributes (time, space, tone, and topic) of George Bush and John Kerry's websites. Framing research then continued with Twitter, Facebook, and Wikipedia. Goodnow (2013) studied Romney and Obama's Facebook timeline photographs to understand what they communicated to potential voters. The results showed that Romney's campaign posted twice as many images of him. Because Obama was already president, he did not have to work as hard as Romney to establish credibility. In addition, Romney's photos included images of war heroes and firefighters, while Obama's images included common people such as a janitor. Grabe and Bucy (2009) suggested three frames through which politicians try to encourage voters to view them: the Ideal Candidate, the Populist Campaigner, and the Sure Loser.

Wasike (2013) conducted a content analysis of 950 tweets to examine which frames social media editors choose for the articles posted via Twitter. The results showed that TV social media editors were more likely to personalize their tweets than their print news counterparts. In terms of the themes, TV social media editors posted more technology framed stories, while print social media editors emphasized human interest, conflict, and economic impact frames the most. The rationale for the dominance of technology stories lies in the fact that most Twitter users are young and tech-savvy (Wasike, 2013). Another framing study related to Twitter has been conducted. Hemphill, Culotta, and Heston (2013) examined how members of the U.S. Congress use hashtags, to what extent politicians participate in framing, and which issues received the most framing efforts. They found that healthcare and the economy received the most framing efforts. These results actually were not surprising considering that these two issues are some of the ones dividing Republicans and Democrats.

Chung and Cho (2013) evaluated the roles of mass media messages and social network sites in the Middle East by analyzing coverage of for U.S. newspapers. They discovered that all newspapers referred to Facebook as a major political tool for change in the Middle East. However, there were differences in the themes of each paper covered. For example, the *Washington Post*'s coverage was mostly thematic, including in-depth stories and professional comments, while *USA Today* did not cover the developments much. The *International Herald Tribune* paid close attention to the issue, focusing on the SNSs' effects and functions in various authoritarian countries. The *New York Times* covered the role of SNSs in the growth of a democratic consciousness under the authoritarian regimes.

Framing theory has also been used to understand how the Occupy Wall Street protests were framed. Researchers (DeLuca, Lawson, & Sun, 2012) have argued that Twitter, Facebook, and YouTube create new contexts for activism that did not exist in traditional media. It took much longer for newspapers to pick up the stream of stories about Occupy Wall

Street—unlike Twitter and Facebook which were following and giving support to the protesters from Day One. DeLuca et al. (2012) found that right- and left-leaning political blogs framed the protest in different ways. The right-leaning blogosphere framed the protesters as "dirty and dangerous" (p. 495), and were generally unsympathetic. The left-leaning blogosphere supported the movement, emphasizing its impact on educating the public about economic inequality in the United States (DeLuca et al., 2012; Yglesias, 2011).

One study has focused on how Wikipedia references have been framed in national newspapers. Messner and South (2011) used framing theory in their content analysis of Wikipedia references in five U.S. newspapers (the *New York Times*, the *Washington Post*, the *Wall Street Journal*, *USA Today*, and the *Christian Science Monitor*). Most articles referencing Wikipedia were published in the *New York Times*, followed by the *Washington Post*. Fifty-five percent of the articles were framed neutrally, 28 percent were positive, and 17 percent were framed negatively. Messner and South (2011) concluded that by treating Wikipedia as a positive phenomenon and an accurate source of information, U.S. newspapers are helping to legitimize the online encyclopedia.

Kwon and Moon (2009) examined cross-national differences in framing by analyzing U.S. and Korean newspapers and blogs about the Virginia Tech campus shooting. While they did not find many cultural differences, the results suggested that the most important concern of the Korean public was the fact that the gunman was "a member of our group." For Americans, it did not matter that he was "one of us" (p. 284). According to Kwon and Moon (2009), the Korean newspapers and public perceived the issue as a threat to national reputation, which might indicate that the nation is inclined to understand the issue from their collectivistic perspective.

Several studies have shown that social media provide an alternative way to frame events by allowing different voices to be heard and marginalized groups to be seen. Hamdy and Gomaa (2012) and Khamis and Mahmoud (2013) have examined how social media framed the demonstrations and political elections in Egypt. Hamdy and Gomaa (2012) found that, unlike newspapers that used the conflict frame as the dominant frame, social media adopted the human interest frame while covering demonstrations in 2011. Khamis and Mahmoud (2013) used a content analysis of the Facebook pages of the top five candidates in the Egyptian presidential race of 2012 to understand how they used them to frame their own images online before, during, and after the elections. Ironically, the candidate who became Egypt's first democratically elected president had the lowest number of Facebook posts (Khamis & Mahmoud, 2013). This indicates that other factors, not just social media, influence political outcomes (see chapter 4 for more information about other factors contributing to the Arab Spring).

CULTIVATION THEORY

Cultivation theory (Gerbner & Gross, 1976) suggests that mass communication, especially television, cultivates certain beliefs about reality. Because of the violent programs on television, heavy television viewers perceive the world to be more violent than it actually is. Although several scholars and media professionals have argued that the Internet may contribute to George Gerbner's "mean world syndrome" due to its focus on the impact of television, cultivation theory has not received much of the social media scholars' attention. Another reason is a belief that the audience is not as passive on social media as Gerbner has proposed with television viewers. However, several studies have found that what other people post online might cultivate the perceptions of other audiences who read their stuff. For example, Bautista (2013) argued that there are rumors circling outside, and people are quick to make negative comments not just about the restaurants where they ate, but also the products that they did not like. Other users might be influenced by their comments and not attend the establishment themselves, or not purchase the product that has a negative review.

Meyer (2011) proposed that cultivation theory might be used to explain low body image among women who compare themselves to beauty standards dictated by those media. Meyer argued that the Internet is replacing television as the most pervasive medium today, especially among young adults. However, Meyer (2011) did not find a direct relationship between comparisons and low body image. It is true that they did not use a comparison scale, but rather selective photo sharing, self-esteem, and impression management—so future studies should try to understand the extent to which social media can share our perceptions of beauty and an ideal body image.

SPIRAL OF SILENCE THEORY

According to *spiral of silence theory* (Noelle-Neumann, 1984), people are less willing to speak about an issue if they perceive that the majority does not share their point of view. Those who remain silent do it due to the fear of isolation. One of the assumptions of spiral of silence theory is that individuals always engage in assessing the climate of opinions by receiving information from media and personal observation. If their opinion is not popular, they will not share it. Noelle-Neumann (1984) calls it a "quasi-statistical sense." When people misperceive public opinion, those observations are called "pluralistic ignorance."

Several studies (e.g., Hampton, Rainie, Lu, Dwyer, Shin, & Purcell, 2014; Lee & Kim, 2014; Lemin, 2010) have explored whether social media help with the spiral of silence: do those with minority views feel freer to express their opinions on Facebook and Twitter? It would seem possible that social media might attract individuals who otherwise will not speak up. However, the results seem to support the opposite hypothesis. Hampton et al. (2014) discovered that people behave on social media similarly as they do face to face. The survey was conducted by the Pew Research Center, was nationally representative, and included 1,801 adults. Those who used Facebook and Twitter were more willing to share their views if their friends agreed with them. In other words, the results showed that social media do not provide an alternative channel for those who often remain silent. In fact, when asked if they would discuss the Edward Snowden-National Security Agency story, they felt more comfortable discussing it during a family meal, at a restaurant with friends, or at a community meeting than on Facebook and Twitter. Lemin (2010) similarly concluded that the spiral of silence does not appear to be altered by the nature of the social media environment. This was also true in Lee and Kim's (2007) study that surveyed Korean journalists from different newspaper and broadcast companies to test their willingness to express their opinions about controversial issues on Twitter. Results showed that those journalists perceived to hold a minority view (more conservative) were less likely to voice their opinions than those who perceived themselves to hold popular beliefs.

However, one study (Neill, 2009) found that social media are challenging spiral of silence theory when it comes to the hardcore. Those are individuals who are in the minority but will speak up regardless of the majority view. In the exploratory analysis of GLBT (gay, lesbian, bisexual, transgendered) communities, Neill (2009) found that social media provide them both access to supporters and also to each other. Future studies should focus on other hard-core groups to learn if they take advantage of social media as an alternative way to express themselves and support each other.

SUMMARY

This chapter discussed how traditional mass media theories have been applied to understand social media. The theory that has been most used in the context of social media, primarily blogs and social networking sites, is uses and gratifications. This is not surprising considering that U& G assumed that the media audience is active and will therefore use Twitter, Facebook, or blogs to satisfy their own needs. Although a few studies have suggested that agenda-setting theory could be further revised for the purposes of social media, there is not enough evidence that social media cause the widespread reversed agenda-setting, or influence the traditional media coverage (newspapers, magazines, radio, and television). One of the main issues with social media remains its credibility question. Anybody can be citizen journalists and post information on their own social media account. Social media, however, have contributed to the intermedia agenda-setting by influencing each other's coverage. Social media also served an important function in agenda building, often as a source of information for traditional media. One theory that should be further used in relation to social media is spiral of silence. More research is needed to understand how "hardcore" (minority) groups use social media to express and organize themselves.

REFERENCES

Armstrong, C. L., & McAdams, M. J. (2011). Blogging the time away? Young adults' motivations for blog use. *Atlantic Journal of Communication, 19*(2), 113-128. doi:10.1080/15456870.2011.561174.

Artwick, S. G. (2012). *Body found on Twitter: The role of alternative sources in social media agenda setting.* Paper presented at the International Communication Association conference, Washington, DC.

Bautista, V. (2013). *How can cultivation theory be applied in social media.* Retrieved from http://www.socialmediatoday.com/content/how-protect-brands-against-mean-world-syndrome-social-media.

Bichard, S. L. (2006). Building blogs: A multi-dimensional analysis of the distribution of frames on the 2004 presidential candidate web sites. *Journalism & Mass Communication Quarterly, 83*(2), 329-345. doi:10.1177/107769900608300207.

Borah, P. (2014). Does it matter where you read the news story? Interaction of incivility and news frames in the political blogosphere. *Communication Research, 41*, 809-827. doi:10.1177/0093650212449353.

Cappella, J., & Jamieson, K. (1997). *Spiral of cynicism: The press and the public good.* New York, NY: Oxford University Press.

Chen, G. (2011). Tweet this: A uses and gratifications perspective on how active twitter use gratifies a need to connect with others. *Computers in Human Behavior, 27*(2), 755-762. doi:10.1016/j.chb.2010.10.023.

Chung, J. C., & Cho, S. (2013). News coverage analysis of SNSs and the Arab Spring: Using mixed methods. *Global Media Journal: American Edition*, 1-26.

DeLuca, K., Lawson, S., & Sun, Y. (2012). Occupy Wall Street on the public screens of social media: The many framings of the birth of a protest movement. *Communication, Culture, and Critique, 5*, 483-509. doi:10.1111/j.1753-9137.2012.01141.x.

Drezner, D., & Farrell, H. (2004). *The power and politics of blogs.* Presented at the American Political Science Association.

Gerbner, G., & Gross, L. (1976). Living with television: The violence profile. *Journal of Communication, 26*, 172–199. doi:10.1111/j.1460-2466.1976.tb01397.x.

Goode, L. (2009). Social news, citizen journalism and democracy. *New Media & Society, 11*(8), 287-305. doi:10.1177/1461444809341393.

Goodnow, T. (2013). Facing off: A comparative analysis of Obama and Romney Facebook timeline photographs. *American Behavioral Scientist, 57*, 1584-1595. doi:10.1177/0002764213489013.

Grabe, M. E., & Bucy, E. P. (2009). *Image bite politics: News and the visual framing of elections.* Oxford, UK: Oxford University Press.

Groshek, J., & Groshek Clough, M. (2013). Agenda trending: Reciprocity and the predictive capacity of social networking sites in intermedia agenda setting across topics over time. *Media and Communication, 1*, 15-27. doi:10.12924/mac2013.01010015.

Grzywinska, I., & Borden, J. (2014). *The impact of social media on traditional media agenda setting theory—the case study of Occupy Wall Street Movement in USA.* Retrieved from

http://www.academia.edu/7484515/The_impact_of_social_media_on
_traditional_media_agenda_setting_theory._The_case_study_of_Occupy
_Wall_Street_Movement_in_USA.

Guillory, B. (2007). *A framing analysis of science and technology weblogs: How is science presented by commentators?* Paper presented at the annual meeting of the International Communication Association, San Francisco.

Hamdy, N., & Gomaa, E. (2012). Framing the Egyptian uprising in Arabic language newspapers and social media. *Journal of Communication, 62,* 195-211. doi:10.1111/j.1460-2466.2012.01637.x.

Hampton, K. N., Rainie, L., Lu, W., Dwyer, M., Shin, I., & Purcell, K. (2014). *Social media and the spiral of silence.* Pew Research Center. Retrieved from http://www.pewinternet.org/2014/08/26/social-media-and-the-spiral-of-silence/.

Hanson, G., & Haridakis, P. (2008). YouTube users watching and sharing the news: A uses and gratifications approach. *Journal of Electronic Publishing, 11*(3), 6. doi:10.3998/3336451.0011.305.

Haridakis, P., & Hanson, G. (2009). Social interaction and co-viewing with YouTube: Blending mass communication reception and social connection. *Journal of Broadcasting & Electronic Media, 53*(2), 317-335. doi:10.1080/08838150902908270.

Hemphill, L., Culotta, A., and Heston, M. (2013). *Framing in social media: How the U.S. Congress uses Twitter hashtags to frame political issues.* Retrieved from http://papers.ssrn.com/sol3/papers.cfm?abstract_id=2317335">http://papers.ssrn.com/sol3/papers.cfm?abstract_id=2317335.

Hicks, A., Comp, S., Horovitz, J., Hovarter, M., Miki, M., & Bevan, J. L. (2012). Why people use Yelp.com: An exploration of uses and gratifications. *Computers in Human Behavior, 28,* 2274–2279. doi:10.1016/j.chb.2012.06.034.

Iyengar, S. (1991). *Is anyone responsible? How television frames political issues.* Chicago, IL: University of Chicago Press.

Johnson, P. R., & Yang, S. (2009). Uses and gratifications of Twitter: An examination of user motives and satisfaction of Twitter use. Paper presented at the Communication Technology Division of the annual convention of the Association for Education in Journalism and Mass Communication in Boston, MA.

Katz, E., Blumler, J. G., & Gurevitch, M. (1973). Uses and gratifications research. *The Public Opinion Quarterly, 37,* 509-623. doi:10.1086/268109.

Kaye, B. K. (2005). It's a blog, blog, blog, blog world: Users and uses of weblogs. *Atlantic Journal of Communication, 13,* 73-95. doi:10.1207/s15456889ajc1302_2.

Kaye, B. K. (2010). Going to the blogs: Exploring the uses and gratifications of blogs. *Atlantic Journal of Communication, 18,* 194-210. doi:10.1080/15456870.2010.505904.

Khamis, S., & Mahmoud, A. (2013). Facebooking the Egyptian elections: Framing the 2012 presidential race. *Journal of Arab & Muslim Media Research, 6,* 133-154.

Kim, S.-T., & Lee, Y.-H. (2007). New functions of Internet mediated agenda-setting: Agenda-rippling and reversed agenda-setting. *Korean Journal of Journalism and Communication Studies, 50,* 175–205.

Kowai-Bell, N., Guadagno, R., Little, T., Preiss, N., & Hensley, R. (2011). Rate my expectations: How online evaluations of professors impact students' perceived control. *Computers in Human Behavior, 27,* 1862-1867. doi:10.1016/j.chb.2011.04.009.

Krause, A. E., North, A. C., & Heritage, B. (2014). The uses and gratifications of using Facebook music listening applications. *Computers in Human Behavior, 39,* 71-77. doi:10.1016/j.chb.2014.07.001.

Kwak, H., Lee, C., Park, H., & Moon, S. (2010). *What is Twitter, a social network or a news media?* Paper presented at WWW 2010, Raleigh, North Carolina.

Kwon, K. H., & Moon, S. (2009). The bad guy is one of us: Framing comparison between the U.S. and Korean newspapers and blogs about the Virginia Tech shooting. *Asian Journal of Communication, 19,* 270-288. doi:10.1080/01292980903038998.

Lee, N. Y., & Kim, Y. (2014). The spiral of silence and journalists' outspokenness on Twitter. *Asian Journal of Communication, 24,* 262-278. doi:10.1080/01292986.2014.885536.

Lemin, D. (2010). *Public opinion in the social media era: Toward a new understanding of the spiral of silence*. ProQuest, UMI Dissertation Publishing.

Lopez-Escobar, E., Llamas, J. P., McCombs, M., & Lennon, F. R. (1998). Two levels of agenda setting among advertising and news in the 1995 Spanish elections. *Political Communication, 15*, 225-38. doi:10.1080/10584609809342367.

McCombs, M. (2004). *Setting the agenda: The mass media and public opinion*. Cambridge, UK: Polity.

McCombs, M., & Shaw, D. L. (1972). The agenda-setting function of the mass media. *Public Opinion Quarterly, 36*, 176-185. doi:10.1086/267990.

McQuail, D., Blumler, J. G., & Brown, J. R. (1972). The television audience: Revised perspective. In D. McQuail (Ed.), *Sociology of mass communications* (pp. 135–165). Harmondsworth, UK: Penguin.

Meraz, S. (2009). Is there an elite hold? Traditional media to social media agenda setting influence in blog networks. *Journal of Computer-Mediated Communication, 14*, 682–707. doi:10.1111/j.1083-6101.2009.01458.x.

Messner, M., & Distaso, M. (2008). How traditional media and weblogs use each other as sources. *Journalism Studies, 9*, 447-463. doi:10.1080/14616700801999287.

Messner, M., & South, J. (2011). Legitimizing Wikipedia. *Journalism Practice, 5*(2), 145-160. doi:10.1080/17512786.2010.506060.

Meyer, M. E. (2011). *Image management on Facebook: Impression management, self-esteem and the cultivation theory*. Presented to the Faculty of the Graduate School of the University of Texas at Austin.

Mosemghvdlishvili, L., & Jansz, J. (2013). Framing and praising Allah on YouTube: Exploring user-created videos about Islam and the motivations for producing them. *New Media and Society, 15*(4), 482-500. doi:10.1177/1461444812457326.

Mull, I. R., & Lee, S. (2014). "PIN" pointing the motivational dimensions behind Pinterest. *Computers in Human Behavior, 33*, 192-200. doi:10.1016/j.chb.2014.01.011.

Nardi, B. A., Schiano, D. J., Gumbrecht, M., & Swartz, L. (2004). Why we blog. *Communications of the ACM, 47*, 41-46.

Neill, S. A. (2009). *The alternate channel: How social media is challenging the spiral of silence theory in GLBT communities of color*. Unpublished master's thesis. Retrieved from http://www.american.edu/soc/communication/upload/09-neill.pdf.

Noelle-Neumann, E. (1984). *The spiral of silence: A theory of public opinion—Our social skin*. Chicago: University of Chicago Press.

Ragas, M. W., & Kiousis, S. (2010). Intermedia agenda-setting and political activism: MoveOn.org and the 2008 Presidential election. *Mass Communication and Society, 13*, 560–583. doi:10.1080/15205436.2010.515372.

Russell Neuman, W. W., Guggenheim, L., Mo Jang, S. S., & Bae, S. (2014). The dynamics of public attention: Agenda-setting theory meets big data. *Journal of Communication, 64*(2), 193-214. doi:10.1111/jcom.12088.

Sayre, B., Bode, L., Shah, D., Wilcox, D., & Shah, C. (2010). Agenda setting in a digital age: Tracking attention to California Proposition 8 in social media, online news, and conventional news. *Policy & Internet, 2*, 7–32. doi:10.1102/1944-2866.1040.

Semetko, H. & Valkenburg, P. (2000). Framing European politics: A content analysis of press and television news. *Journal of Communication, 50*(2), 93-109. doi:10.1111/j.1460-2466.2000.tb02843.x.

Sheldon, P. (2008). The relationship between unwillingness to communicate and students' Facebook use. *Journal of Media Psychology, 20*, 67-75. doi:10.1027/1864-1105.20.2.6.

Shoemaker, P. J., & Reese, S. D. (2014). *Mediating the message in the 21st century: A media sociology perspective*. New York, NY: Allyn and Bacon.

Smock, A. D., Ellison, N. B., Lampe, C., & Wohn, D. (2011). Facebook as a toolkit: A uses and gratification approach to unbundling feature use. *Computers in Human Behavior, 27*(6), 2322-2329. doi:10.1016/j.chb.2011.07.011.

Song, I., LaRose, R., Eastin, M. S., & Lin, C. A. (2004). Internet gratifications and internet addiction: On the uses and abuses of new media. *Cyberpsychology & Behavior, 7*, 384–393. doi:10.1089/cpb.2004.7.384.

Volders, S. (2013). *Agenda-setting theory in political discourse on Twitter*. Master's thesis. Retrieved from http://arno.uvt.nl/show.cgi?fid=130756.

Wasike, B. S. (2013). Framing news in 140 characters: How social media editors frame the news and interact with audiences via Twitter. *Global Media Journal—Canadian Edition, 6*(1), 5-23.

Yglesias, M. (2011, October 13).Wonky protest sign highlights growing inequality. *Think Progress*. [Web log post]. Retrieved from http://thinkprogress.org/yglesias/2011/10/13/343633/wonky-protest-sign-highlights-growing-inequality.

THREE

Psychology of Social Media

This chapter focuses on personality psychology and individual differences of people who use social media. "Personality is a leading factor in understanding why people behave the way they do on the Internet" (Amichai-Hamburger, 2002, p. 1290). As people spend more time on social media, it is important to understand who uses these sites. The following chapter provides an overview of the media psychology research as it relates to users and nonusers of social media.

Personality traits that are theoretically linked to online self-presentation include narcissism, extroversion, self-efficacy, the need to belong, and the need for popularity. When it comes to social media, researchers have particularly focused on narcissism and extroversion, as these directly relate to social media use. Other personality constructs studied in relation to social media include shyness, loneliness, and sensation seeking.

SELF-PRESENTATION

In his book *The Presentation of Self in Everyday Life*, Erving Goffman (1959) described social life by using theatrical metaphors. According to the metaphors, we are all performers who take on unique roles in different situations. We have a "front stage behavior" and a "back stage behavior." When we follow formal societal rules, we are on the front stage playing a "role." An example would be how we behave at work. Our back stage behavior, however, is more informal and includes interaction with friends (Goffman, 1959).

Goffman's self-presentation techniques have been applied in studies looking at self-presentation online. Walther (1992) used the term selective self-presentation to describe how, in the absence of nonverbal cues, more emphasis is placed on linguistic cues. Reduced cues and asynchronous

computer-mediated communication contribute to selective self-presentation (Walther, 1996). This might include different activities on social media, such as posting status updates or tweets, joining groups, liking
pages, as well as sharing personal photographs on Facebook, Twitter,
and Instagram. Not only do the users have an option to choose a profile
photo for themselves, but they can allow others to tag them in photos that
they did not take themselves. With the privacy settings, users can also
limit who can tag a photo of them on Facebook and thus prevent an
embarrassing photo from showing up on their timeline. By creating online self-presentation, users have the opportunity to decide which information they want on their Facebook, Twitter, or Instagram account. In
other words, they can manage their self-presentations more successfully
than in face-to-face interactions (Ellison, Heino, & Gibbs, 2006).

Online media differs from other media types by allowing participants
to co-construct their own environment, primarily through social interaction (Manago, Graham, Greenfield, & Salimkhan, 2008). Research has
also found that adolescents often experiment with their online identities,
pretending to be someone else or just realizing aspects of themselves that
are limited in their offline lives (Manago et al., 2008; Greenfield, Gross,
Subrahmanyam, Suzuki, & Tynes, 2006). The appeal of social networking
sites is the capacity to present ourselves in an indefinite number of ways
(Manago et al., 2008). This is the reason many (e.g., Buffardi & Campbell,
2008; Leung, 2013; Mehdizadeh, 2010) have argued that narcissists prefer
online communities consisting of *shallow relationships*, as they have complete control over their self-presentation. Social media offer a "nonymous" (the opposite of anonymous) online setting that provides an
ideal environment for the expression of the "hoped-for possible self," or
rather a socially desirable identity that an individual wants to establish
(Mehdizadeh, 2010; Zhao, Grasmuck, & Martin, 2008).

Narcissism

Narcissism is a personality trait reflecting an inflated self-concept (Buffardi & Campbell, 2008), a need for admiration, and an exaggerated sense
of self-importance (Oltmanns, Emery, & Taylor, 2006). Narcissists generally think that they are better than others, unique, and special (Leung,
2013). Originally, Raskin and Hall (1979) developed a 223-item inventory
to measure the extent of a narcissistic personality. In the subsequent
study, Raskin and Terry (1988) proposed seven dimensions of narcissism:
authority, self-sufficiency, superiority, exhibitionism, exploitativeness,
vanity, and entitlement. Ackermann et al. (2011) proposed a narcissism
model constituting of three factors: leadership/authority, grandiose exhibitionism, and entitlement/exploitativeness. Leung (2013) and Foster and
Campbell (2007) discovered four dimensions of narcissistic personality:
feeling authoritative or superior, exhibitionism, exploitativeness, and

hunger for vanity. Of all the narcissistic types Leung (2013) found, exhibitionists seek all forms of social media. Exhibitionists use social media to show affection, to express their negative feelings, and for recognition. Those who feel superior are motivated by their cognitive needs, while those with a vain personality seek recognition and attention (Leung, 2013).

Research suggests that Facebook is appealing to narcissists. The most important indicators of narcissism on Facebook are the main profile photo and the number of social contacts (Buffardi & Campbell, 2008). Narcissism is related to how often students post personal photographs on Facebook, as well as how often they comment and like on their friends' photos (Sheldon, 2015). Narcissists are highly motivated to choose profile photos that emphasize their attractiveness (Kapidzic, 2013). When it comes to Facebook status updates, researchers argue (Walther, 2007; Winter, Neubaum, Eimler, Gordon, Theil, Herrmann, Meinert, & Kramer, 2014) that they are a perfect way to manage impressions of their self, as individuals can carefully select what to write for their status. Narcissism was the most important predictor of the frequency of status updates (Winter et al., 2014). Higher degrees of narcissism led to deeper self-disclosures, which Winter et al. interpreted as a strategy to increase attention or recipients' "liking" of the sender.

Mendelson and Papacharissi (2010) studied collective narcissism in college students' Facebook photo galleries. They argued that students are consciously uploading photos on Facebook, selecting certain subjects and events such as high school proms, sporting events, Halloween parties, St. Patrick's Day, as well as road trips. Many photographs documented rituals and important milestones, including birthdays, holidays, and weddings. When it comes to subjects in the photos, most photos portrayed same-sex groups of friends. Very few pictures included students' families. Contextual elements and backgrounds were deemphasized. In terms of behavior, it is almost always intentional and formal. Many women posed provocatively, sometimes joking with friends and kissing each other. Aesthetically, most photos were centered with subjects looking at the camera. Many photos also included self-shots or "selfies." Comments on the photos function as a reinforcement of group cohesiveness.

Extroversion

Extroversion is another construct that has received a lot of scholarly attention. Extroversion is defined as an individual's tendency to be outgoing and engage in social activities (Winter et al., 2014). Carl Jung first proposed that personality characteristics like introversion and extroversion play major roles when it comes to one's psychological functions and communication behavior. According to Jung, extroverts in general are sociable, outgoing, compatible, and fit well into society, whereas introverts often have the complete opposite attributes (Acar, 2008). Eysenck (1967) stated that extroversion is one of the most important personality traits that determine an individual's socialization process. Extroverts have been found to be active, assertive, sensation seeking, carefree, dominant, or venturesome (Eysenck, Eysenck, & Barrett, 1985). McCroskey and Richmond (1990) saw extroversion as an antecedent to (un)willingness to communicate (Acar, 2008).

Researchers who study how introversion/extroversion influences online friendship formation came up with two different hypotheses explaining the relationship between extroversion and social media behavior. The rich-get-richer hypothesis states that the Internet primarily benefits extroverted individuals (Kraut, Kiesler, Boneva, et al., 2002). The *social compensation* hypothesis, by contrast, proposes that the Internet benefits introverts more, since it allows them to compensate for the lack of interpersonal contacts (McKenna & Bargh, 2000; Valkerburg & Peter, 2007). When it comes to social media, researchers have found more support for the rich-get-richer hypothesis (Ong et al., 2011; Sheldon, 2008; Utz, Tanis, & Vermeulen, 2012). For many extroverts Facebook is an extension of their social life (Ryan & Xenos, 2011). Facebook users (compared to nonusers) score higher on extroversion (Ryan & Xenos, 2011). They use Facebook to supplement offline relationships (Seidman, 2013). Some elements on Facebook in particular appeal to extroverts such as status updates, the number of Facebook friends, and having a more animated profile picture (Utz, 2010). Extroverted individuals belong to more Facebook groups (Ross et al., 2009). One possible reason for Facebook being more appealing to extroverts might be the fact that Facebook is not as anonymous as the chat rooms and forum boards previously studied. Facebook friends often know each other in real life.

There are, however, inconsistent findings when it comes to the relationship between narcissism and social networking. McKinney, Kelly, and Duran (2012), for example, did not find a significant relationship between narcissism and the frequency of using Facebook to post about oneself. In their study of college students, narcissism was positively related to using Twitter to send tweets about oneself. The authors argued that Twitter might be the perfect place for narcissists because individuals can send a short, 140-character message instantaneously. However, they also acknowledged that SNSs might simply be just one way young adults communicate. They share information about themselves not because they are narcissistic, but because they have a positive attitude about sharing such information. In a more recent study, Davenport, Bergman, Bergman, and Fearrington (2014) found that narcissistic college students prefer to post content on Twitter, while narcissistic adults prefer to post content on Facebook. Their findings indicate the importance of accounting for generational differences when studying social media relationships with personality traits. Millennials grew up with Facebook, but they generally use

Twitter more than the Baby Boomers who are still using Facebook cautiously in order to leave positive impressions to others.

In terms of generational differences, Twenge, Konrath, Foster, Keith, Campbell, and Bushman (2008) found that today's college students score substantially higher on the Narcissism Personality Inventory than did their peers from 20 years ago. They argued that these numbers are consistent with previous studies finding increases in other individualistic traits such as assertiveness, agency, self-esteem, and extroversion. While many of these traits are positive, it is argued that the benefits are only short-term. In the long run, narcissism is related to troubled romantic relationships (Campbell, Foster, & Finkel, 2002) and aggression (Bushman & Baumeister, 1998).

Shyness and Loneliness

Shyness is another construct that has received scholars' attention. *Shyness* has been defined as "discomfort or inhibition in interpersonal situations that interferes with pursuing one's interpersonal or professional goals" (Henderson, Zimbardo, & Carducci, 2001, p. 1522). Because of the missing nonverbal cues, some studies have suggested that shyness might be associated with increased Internet usage (Mesch, 2001; Morahan-Martin & Schumacher, 2003). Orr et al. (2009) also found that shy users spend more time on Facebook. However, Ryan and Xenos (2011) found no significant relationship between shyness and the frequency of Facebook usage. Sheldon's (2013a) study of 150 college students revealed that shy students have fewer Facebook friends than those who are not shy. Shy students disclose less information to their Facebook friends as opposed to students who are less shy. These findings contradict many previous Internet studies (e.g, Ward & Tracey, 2004) which found that shy people feel more secure in online interactions (the social compensation hypothesis). Again, one of the possible reasons might be that there is less of an opportunity to remain anonymous in a social network environment. Online communities such as chat rooms, blogs, and social networks have different purposes and therefore attract different audiences. Facebook is a social network that connects people who have met outside of the virtual world. It is different from chat rooms where people can hide their identities and therefore feel "liberated" to open up. In fact, Sheldon (2008) found that respondents who feel anxiety and fear in their face-to-face communication use Facebook more to pass time and to avoid feelings of loneliness than other respondents who feel less anxious in face-to-face interactions. Although they had fewer Facebook friends, these individuals still log into Facebook more frequently. One of the explanations Sheldon (2008) gave was that those individuals do not self-disclose on Facebook enough to form new relationships, but they still visit the site more often.

What Sheldon (2008) found is that what happens offline often happens on Facebook as well. In fact, scholars have argued that face-to-face communication could coexist and substitute for computer-mediated communication (CMC) and that CMC can be used as an alternative for face-to-face interactions (Perse & Courtright, 1993; Rubin & Rubin, 1985). Smith and Kollock (1999) argue that individuals do not leave their offline selves behind when they log on to the virtual world, but rather they bring their offline identities with them when they are online. They also utilize their offline identities to shape their online interactions and activities.

Morahan-Martin and Schumacher (2003) surveyed 277 undergraduate Internet users to assess the differences in patterns of Internet use between lonely and non-lonely individuals. They found that lonely individuals use the Internet and e-mail more, and were more likely to use the Internet for emotional support than others. Compared to others, lonely users were more likely to prefer communicating online as opposed to face-to-face communication and reported making online friends more than non-lonely individuals. However, with Facebook usage, that was not the case. Sheldon (2013a) conducted a survey of 150 students at a large southern university to determine the relationship between social loneliness and self-disclosure on Facebook. Social isolation is defined as an absence of a place in an accepting community or the absence of meaningful friendships. Social loneliness usually takes the form of boredom and feelings of exclusion (Weiss, 1973). Sheldon's (2013a) results showed that, overall, socially lonely students disclose on Facebook less frequently than students who are not lonely. Socially lonely individuals in particular self-disclose fewer topics to their Facebook friends than individuals who feel "in tune" with others. This supports the rich-get-richer hypothesis (Kraut et al., 2002).

Since lonely and shy students tend to have problems disclosing on Facebook, it seems that the most popular social network resembles word-of-mouth communication. In fact, that tends to be the nature of social networks in general. Social media are different from newspapers and television, Dicken-Garcia (1998) reports. The Internet places a stronger emphasis on informal, interpersonal conversations than has been true of earlier media outlets. Facebook is largely used for people to stay in touch with their friends. The main motive for its use is relationship maintenance (Sheldon, 2008), which means that it satisfies interpersonal communication needs. Unlike chat rooms and bulletin boards, where users primarily connect with strangers to talk about sports or politics, Facebook is not usually a place where strangers meet and talk without knowing each other's physical appearance. Facebook was created for users who are willing to disclose their personal information to 400 other people who all know each other's names. In other words, the purpose of Facebook is to reach out to our personal social network that we also visit, mail, and telephone. This may explain why shy and lonely students may feel less inclined to disclose there.

Quest for Fame

Psychologists have noted that the reasoning behind broadcasting ourselves via personalized new technologies may not only reflect the societal shift toward individualistic values, but also a quest for fame (Greenwood, 2013). Uhls and Greenfield (2012) define a desire for fame as "a motive or behavior to seek either positive or negative public recognition on a large scale beyond one's immediate network of friends, community, and family, independent of accomplishments in a specific endeavor" (p. 316). In fact, according to uses and gratifications theory, one of the psychological needs individuals have is the need to feel seen and valued (Greenwood, 2013). Uhls and Greenfield's (2012) focus groups with 20 children (9 girls, 11 boys) between 10 and 12 years of age revealed that fame was the number one cultural value in the preadolescent sample. Eight out of 20 children (40 percent) listed fame as their top choice for what they wanted in their future. The reasoning behind this was a connection to money and attention. They argued that a potential synergy exists between observing the fame-oriented content of popular TV shows and enacting those values by posting online videos. On YouTube, people can post videos of themselves and are able to reach a broad audience, thus receiving real feedback concerning their own fame (Uhls & Greenfield, 2012). Uhls and Greenfield argued that even the site's tag line, "Broadcast Yourself," encourages just that.

A perfect example of "Instafame" or a social media celebrity is Benjamin Lasnier, a teenage boy from Denmark, who achieved fame almost entirely through Instagram and YouTube. Lasnier started posting his own "selfies" on Instagram, and, due to his resemblance to Justin Bieber, people began to like the photos. As of November 2014, Lasnier has 5.4 million followers on Facebook and 1.2 million followers on Instagram. Despite wide criticism of his musical talent, Sony signed a contract with Lasnier. Today he has his own recorded album as well as a line of merchandise. Lasnier is a perfect example of what Uhls and Greenfield (2012) observed in their study. Anybody can become a celebrity through social media. But social media can change the way we look at fame as well.

Self-Disclosure

Studies have suggested that the Internet provides an opportunity for shy individuals to disclose more online than in face-to-face interactions, as computer-mediated channels provide an opportunity for both anonymous and delayed interactions. Researchers have tested shy individuals' addiction to the Internet and online self-disclosure (Peter, Valkenburg, &

Schouten, 2005). However, few studies have examined how those individuals privately disclose to their Facebook friends. Self-disclosure is viewed as a major factor in the development, maintenance, and deterioration of a relationship. Self-disclosure is an important aspect of friendships and measures the intensity of a relationship (Levinger & Rands, 1985).

While the concept of self-disclosure has mainly been studied in the context of face-to-face interactions, with the advent of new technologies this notion has been transferred to a computer-mediated context as well (e.g., Joinson, 2001). Self-disclosure is defined as the process of revealing personal information about oneself (e.g., Berg & Derlega, 1987) to another individual(s). Altman and Taylor (1973) developed social penetration theory to describe how people disclose face to face in order to develop relationships. They suggested two dimensions of self-disclosure: (a) "breadth," or the amount of information disclosed, and (b) "depth," or the intimacy of self-disclosure. They believed that in initial stages, relationships have narrow breadth and shallow depth. As relationships move more toward intimacy, a wider range of topics is discussed (breadth), with several of the topics to be intimately discussed (depth) (Altman & Taylor, 1987). Due to limited nonverbal and contextual cues, researchers (Cho, 2006; Walther, 1992; 1996) have argued that self-disclosure is important for the formation of online relationships in a computer-mediated environment.

Unlike most of the previous research, which found that shy people feel more secure in online interactions (e.g., Scharlott & Christ, 1995; Sheeks & Birchmeier, 2007; Stritzke, Nguyen, & Durkin, 2004; Turkle, 1995; Ward & Tracey, 2004), Sheldon (2013a) found no evidence that this was the case. Shy and lonely individuals do not use Facebook to compensate for the lack of face-to-face interactions, nor for the lack of Facebook friends. In Sheldon's (2013a) study, shy and socially lonely students disclose to their close Facebook friends less than do students who are less shy and lonely. Shy students also have fewer Facebook friends and fewer face-to-face friends than individuals who are less shy. It is possible that shy students do not self-disclose enough to develop new relationships as they fear disapproval, which then generates anxiety. Studies (e.g., Baumeister & Leary, 1995) have actually found that shy people want to form relationships with others and have as much a need as non-shy people to belong. However, if they do not have a large offline network of friends, they do not have many friends on Facebook either. Findings from Orr et al. (2009) also support the notion that shy users have fewer Facebook friends.

Body Image

Few empirical studies (e.g., Lee, 2014; Rutledge, Gillmor, & Gillen, 2013) have been conducted to examine the links between Facebook and body image. Body image is a multidimensional construct that encompasses how individuals think, feel, and act in regards to their bodies (Thompson, Heinberg, Altabe, & Tantleff-Dunn, 1999). Previous research indicates that late adolescence and the transition to university life are periods of increased risk for eating problems for both men and women (Dickstein, 1989; Lorenzen, Grieve, & Thomas, 2004; Striegel-Moore, Silberstein, Frensch, & Rodin, 1989). One of the most common risks for eating pathology is body dissatisfaction. About 80 percent of college women say that have been dissatisfied with their bodies at some point of time (Fitzsimmons-Craft, 2011). This often results from social comparison to peers (Sheldon, 2013b). According to Festinger's *social comparison theory* (1954), humans are naturally driven to compare themselves to others. While an upward comparison includes a comparison to supermodels in mass media, a lateral comparison is a comparison to fellow peer groups (Sohn, 2010). This can especially happen on Facebook. Although few studies have examined how social media sites such as Facebook might encourage social comparison, Rutledge et al. (2013) found that with Facebook being a visual medium, it may be more appealing to those who are concerned with their appearance because it allows them to construct the image that they wish to portray to the public. Students who have more Facebook friends have more positive evaluations of their appearances. Rutledge et al. explained this as one of the reasons for posting photos on Facebook. Those who have more friends expect more positive comments on their photos. Results showed that those who spent less time on Facebook were also more concerned with their looks. They might fear portraying unattractive images. Lee (2014) examined social comparison orientation (SCO) on Facebook and studied how college students' personality characteristics (e.g., social comparison orientation, self-esteem, self-uncertainty, and self-consciousness) influence a person's social comparison frequency on Facebook. Students who scored higher on social comparison orientation were more likely to compare themselves to others on Facebook. Lee defined SCO as "the extent to which individuals pay attention to and base their own behavior on the way others behave" (p. 254). In addition, Lee (2014) found that students who were less certain about themselves had low self-esteem and used Facebook more frequently, presumably in order to compare themselves with others on Facebook.

The limitation of social comparison studies is that most people are reluctant to admit that they compare themselves to others (Lee, 2014). Most studies on social comparison are cross-sectional, thus preventing us from making causal conclusions.

Digital Divide

In 2009, 15 percent of the participants in the university student population were not Facebook users. In 2013 (Ljepava, Orr, Locke, & Ross,

2013), 8 percent of the college student participants still did not have Facebook accounts. It is obvious that the number of non-users is declining. Very few studies (Ljepava et al., 2013; Ryan & Xenos, 2011; Sheldon, 2012) have focused on personality characteristics of Facebook non-users. Ryan and Xenos (2011) concluded that non-users were less narcissistic, less extroverted, more conscientious, and more socially lonely than Facebook users. Sheldon (2012) also found that non-users are significantly older, more shy and more lonely, less socially active, and less prone to sensation seeking activities. Counter to previous findings (Ryan & Xenos, 2011) showing that non-users were less narcissistic, Ljepava et al.'s (2013) study revealed that non-users scored higher on covert narcissism (measured with the Hypersensitive Narcissism Scale), which indicates that they are less inclined to publicly expose their narcissism.

SOCIAL MEDIA AND WELL-BEING

Researchers have studied the impact of social media technology on individuals' psycho-social well-being. While potential mental health benefits include an increase in social support and social capital (Ellison, Steinfield, & Lampe, 2007), negative consequences can include social isolation and a decrease in face-to-face interactions, as well as social media addiction and attention deficit.

In his study of social media users in Norway, Brandtzæg (2012) argued that the media-fueled "antisocial networking" claims about negative social implications of social network sites are in fact not true. Brandtzæg (2012) surveyed a representative sample of 2,000 Norwegian online users (aged 15–75 years) in three annual waves from 2008, 2009, and 2010. His study found a significantly higher score among SNS users in comparison to non-users in three out of four social capital dimensions: face-to-face interactions, number of acquaintances, and bridging capital. In other words, social network sites can help strengthen bonds with family, friends, and acquaintances. These results were similar to those of Ellison et al. (2007) who found that the use of Facebook is associated with the maintenance and creation of social capital. Social capital is defined as the resources accumulated through relationships among people (our social network). "Bridging social capital" includes "weak ties" or loose connections between individuals who may provide useful information or new perspectives but typically not emotional support. "Bonding social capital" is built through tightly knit, emotionally close relationships (family and close friends). For many college students, Ellison et al. (2007) found that Facebook is a way to keep in touch with their high school friends. In fact, students low in self-esteem and with low satisfaction gain in bridging social capital if they use Facebook more intensely (the poor-get-richer). Other benefits of social capital include emotional support, better mental and physical health, lower crime rates (neighbors looking after each other), higher self-esteem, and higher life satisfaction.

Earlier, Brandtzæg (2010) identified five types of SNS users: Sporadics (low level users of SNSs), Lurkers (people who use SNSs but do not contribute or interact), Socializers (people who use SNSs mainly for social interaction with friends and family), Debaters (people who use SNSs mainly for debating and discussion), and Advanced (people who use SNSs frequently for almost all purposes including socializing, debating, and contributing). Socializers report higher levels of social capital compared to other user types, supporting the "rich-get-richer" hypothesis (Brandtzæg, 2012). Sporadics and Lurkers report less social capital than other types. Over time, however, the study showed an increase in weak ties among Debaters and Advanced users who often engage in discussions and meetings with new people in SNSs. However, SNS users reported more loneliness than non-users. Brandtzæg (2012) argued that this might be due to the lesser frequency of meaningful relationships for males in SNSs, as most studies show that SNSs seem to be a much more important tool for socializing among females in comparison to males (Hargittai, 2007; Sheldon, 2008).

Best, Manktelow, and Taylor (2014) also emphasized that those who have higher quality relationships have a higher well-being. In that sense, online relationships can positively affect individuals' well-being. Social support offered through SNSs and blogs includes increased emotional support, self-disclosure, reduced social anxiety, and belongingness (Best et al., 2014; Duggan, Heath, Lewis, & Baxter, 2012).

A negative relationship between online communication practices and individuals' well-being has also been documented. Rosen, Cheever, and Carrier (2012) coined the term "iDisorder," which is the negative relationship between technology use and psychological health. Other studies have found a relationship between depression and excessive texting, viewing video clips, video gaming, e-mailing, as well as chatting (e.g., Amichai-Hamburger & Ben-Artzi, 2009; Chen & Tzeng, 2010; as cited in Rosen, Whaling, Rab, Carrier, & Cheever, 2013). A number of the studies reported earlier in the chapter have demonstrated the relationship between narcissism and social media use. Narcissism is encouraged and fueled by social networking sites (Bergman, Fearrington, Davenport, & Bergman, 2011). Narcissism is increasing due to the different values of the Net Generation. Besides narcissism, some personality disorders are the result of the obsessive use of social media. For example, Rosen et al.'s (2013) study of 1,143 adults (aged 18 to 65) living in southern California found that multitasking can lead to depression and mania, as well as compulsive and paranoid disorders.

Social media provides new and various ways to hurt victims over and over again. Cyberbullying and cyberstalking are just a few of the concerns for parents. *Cyberbullying* is defined as use of the Internet, cell phones, or other technology to send or post text or images intended to hurt or embarrass another person (Levinson, 2013). Most perpetrators and victims of cyberbullying are teenage girls. Bullies often like to see themselves on YouTube, so they post bullying videos online. One recent event involved a fifteen-year old girl who was assaulted by multiple young men after becoming drunk. After photographs of the assault were posted online, the teen committed suicide. Cyberbullying differs from face-to-face bullying in several ways. First, the online victim may block or terminate interaction with the bully by logging off of the social media site (Menesini & Nocentini, 2009). Second, the potential for empathy among bystanders is reduced in an online environment since they cannot physically see the victim. Because of methodological challenges, few studies have fully examined cyberbullying. Freis and Gurung's (2013) study of the issue aimed to determine what motivates a participant to intervene in an online bullying situation. They studied female users of Facebook, as women often have more involvement in cyberbullying cases (Slonje & Smith, 2008). Results showed that a person high in empathy and high in extroversion is more likely to intervene in a cyberbullying context. However, people are much more likely to use indirect forms of intervention when dealing with a cyberbullying situation. Those who confronted the bully directly scored high in extroversion, while those who tried to change the topic scored high on empathy (Freis & Gurung, 2013). Time spent online may increase the risk of cyberbullying (CB), and both traditional bullying and CB were associated with higher levels of depressive symptoms (Machmutow, Perren, Sticca, & Alsaker, 2012).

Cyberstalking is persistent, unwanted online monitoring or contact with a target, to the point of obsession (Levinson, 2013). Cyberbullying and cyberstalking started with instant messaging and in chat rooms where the perpetrator could stay anonymous. Later they migrated to social media. E-mail, Facebook, FourSquare, and Twitter all allow cyberstalkers to easily track someone's personal life. Most studies actually suggest that the Internet merely provides stalkers with an additional means to exert control over victims (as cited in Welsh & Lavoie, 2012). Most victims who are stalked online have been stalked by the same people offline (Sheridan & Grant, 2007). Spitzberg and his colleagues (Spitzberg, Marshall, & Cupach, 2001) have identified three major categories of cyberstalking: Hyperintimacy, Threat, and Real-Life Transfer. Hyperintimacy includes repeated efforts at cybercommunication with the victims, including sending exaggerated messages of affection or pornographic images. A Threat is an online invasion of privacy and may include intimidating e-mails and Facebook messages. A Real-Life Transfer is a physical intrusion into the victim's life (Welsh & Lavoie, 2012). However, studies show that physical contact between the cyberstalker and victim is rare (Pittaro, 2007).

Welsh and Lavoie (2012) examined the relationship between the sharing of personal information on SNSs, or online disclosiveness, and the risk for cyberstalking. In a sample of 321 female undergraduate students, they found that increasing the amounts of time spent engaging with online social networking, as well as high levels of online disclosure of personal information, contributed to increased risks for cyberstalking.

Researchers have often focused on either positive or negative benefits of online social networking use. Based on the existing research in this area, the reality is that SNS use can affect people both positively and negatively. Vandoninck, d'Haenens, De Cock, and Donoso (2012) emphasized that one key factor associated with increased well-being includes the use of online technology for communicative versus non-communicative purposes. When used for communicative purposes, social media often provide more benefits.

REFERENCES

Acar, A. (2008). Antecedents and consequences of online social networking behavior: The case of Facebook. *Journal of Website Promotion, 3*, 62-83. doi:10.1080/15533610802052654.

Ackerman, R. A., Witt, E. A., Donnellan, M. B., Trzesniewski, K. H., Robins, R. W., & Kashy, D. A. (2011). What does the narcissistic personality inventory really measure? *Assessment, 18*, 67-87. doi:10.1177/1073191110382845.

Amichai-Hamburger, Y. (2002). Internet and personality. *Computers in Human Behavior, 18*, 1-10. doi:10.1016/S0747-5632(01)00034-6.

Amichai-Hamburger, Y., & Ben-Artzi, E. (2009). Depression through technology. *New Scientist, 204*, 28-29.

Altman, I., & Taylor, D. (1973). *Social penetration: The development of interpersonal relationships.* New York: Holt, Rinehart, & Winstron.

Altman, I., & Taylor, D. (1987). Communication in interpersonal relationships: Social penetration processes. In M. Roloff & G. Miller (Eds.), *Interpersonal processes* (pp. 257-277). London, England: Sage Publications.

Baumeister, R. F. & Leary, M. R. (1995). The need to belong: Desire for interpersonal attachments as a fundamental human motivation. *Psychological Bulletin, 117*, 497-529.

Berg, J. H., & Derlega, V. J. (1987). Themes in the study of self-disclosure. In V. J. Derlega & J. H. Berg (Eds.), *Self-disclosure: Theory, research, and therapy* (pp. 1-8). New York: Plenum Press.

Bergman, S. M., Fearrington, M. E., Davenport, S. W., & Bergman, J. Z. (2011). Millennials, narcissism, and social networking: What narcissists do on social networking sites and why. *Personality & Individual Differences, 50*(5), 706-711. doi:10.1016/j.paid.2010.12.022.

Best, P., Manktelow, R., & Taylor, B. (2014). Online communication, social media and adolescent well-being: A systematic narrative review. *Children & Youth Services Review, 41*, 27-36. doi:10.1016/j.childyouth.2014.03.001.

Brandtzæg, P. B. (2010). Towards a unified media-user typology (MUT): A meta-analysis and review of the research literature on media-user typologies. *Computers in Human Behavior, 26*, 940–956. doi:10.1016/j.chb.2010.02.008.

Brandtzæg, P. B. (2012). Social networking sites: Their users and social implications: A longitudinal study. *Journal of Computer-Mediated Communication, 17*, 467-488. doi:10.1111/j.1083-6101.2012.01580.x.

Buffardi, L. E., & Campbell, W. K. (2008). Narcissism and social networking web sites. *Personality and Social Psychology Bulletin, 34,* 1303-1314. doi:10.1177/0146167208320061.

Bushman, B. J., & Baumeister, R. F. (1998). Threatened egotism, narcissism, self-esteem, and direct and displaced aggression: Does self-love or self-hate lead to violence? *Journal of Personality and Social Psychology, 75,* 219-229. doi:10.1016/S0092-6566(02)00502-0.

Campbell, W. K., Foster, C. A., & Finkel, E. J. (2002). Does self-love lead to love for others? A story of narcissistic game playing. *Journal of Personality and Social Psychology, 83,* 340-354. doi:10.1037//0022-3514.83.2.340.

Chen, S. Y., & Tzeng, J. Y. (2010). College female and male heavy Internet users' profiles of practices and their academic grades and psychosocial adjustment. *Cyberpsychology, Behavior, and Social Networking, 13*(3), 257-262.

Cho, S. (2006). *Effects of motivations and gender on adolescents' self-disclosure in online chatting.* Paper presented at the annual meeting of International Communication Association, Dresden, Germany.

Davenport, S. W., Bergman, S. M., Bergman, J. Z., & Fearrington, M. E. (2014). Twitter versus Facebook: Exploring the role of narcissism in the motives and usage of different social media platforms. *Computers in Human Behavior, 32,* 212-220. doi:10.1016/j.chb.2013.12.011.

Dicken-Garcia, H. (1998). Internet and continuing historical discourse. *Journalism and Mass Communication Quarterly, 75,* 19-27. doi: 10.1177/107769909807500105.

Dickstein, L. J. (1989). Current college environments: Do these communities facilitate and foster bulimia in vulnerable students? In L. C. Whitaker and W. N. Davis (Eds.), *The bulimic college student* (pp. 107-133). New York: Hawthorn.

Duggan, J. M., Heath, N. L., Lewis, S. P., & Baxter, A. L. (2012). An examination of the scope and nature of non-suicidal self-injury online activities: Implications for school mental health professionals. *School Mental Health, 4*(1), 56-67. doi:10.1007/s12310-011-9065-6.

Ellison, N., Heino, R., & Gibbs, J. (2006). Managing impressions online: Self-presentation processes in the online dating environment. *Journal of Computer-Mediated Communication, 11,* 415-441. doi:10.1111/j.1083-6101.2006.00020.

Ellison, N., Steinfield, C., & Lampe, C. (2007). The benefits of Facebook "friends": Exploring the relationship between college students' use of online social networks and social capital. *Journal of Computer-Mediated Communication, 12*(4). http://jcmc.indiana.edu/vol12/issue4/ellison.html.

Eysenck, H. J. (1967). *The biological basis of personality.* Springfield, IL: Charles C. Thomas.

Eysenck, S. B., Eysenck, H. J., & Barrett, P. (1985). A revised version of the psychoticism scale. *Personality and Individual Differences, 6,* 21-29. doi:10.1016/0191-8869(85)90026-1.

Festinger, L. (1954). A theory of social comparison processes. *Human Relations, 7,* 117-140. doi:10.1177/001872675400700202.

Fitzsimmons-Craft, E. E. (2011). Social psychological theories of disordered eating in college women: Review and integration. *Clinical Psychological Review, 31,* 1224-1237.

Foster, J. D., & Campbell, W. K. (2007). Are there such things as "Narcissists" in social psychology? A taxometric analysis of the Narcissistic Personality Inventory. *Personality and Individual Differences, 43*(6), 1321-1332. doi:10.1016/j.paid.2007.04.003.

Freis, S. D., & Gurung, R. A. R. (2013). A Facebook analysis of helping behavior in online bullying. *Psychology of Popular Media Culture, 2,* 11-19. doi:10.1037/a0030239.

Goffman, E. (1959). *The presentation of self in everyday life.* New York: Anchor.

Greenfield, P. M., Gross, E. F., Subrahmanyam, K., Suzuki, L. K., & Tynes, B. (2006). Teens on the Internet: Interpersonal connection, identity, and information. In R. Kraut, M. Brynin, & S. Kiesler (Eds.), *Information technology at home* (pp. 185–200). Oxford: Oxford University Press.

Greenwood, D. N. (2013). Fame, Facebook, and Twitter: How attitudes about fame predict frequency and nature of social media use. *Psychology of Popular Media Culture, 2*, 222-236. doi:10.1037/ppm0000013.

Hargittai, E. (2007).Whose space? Differences among users and non-users of social network sites. *Journal of Computer-Mediated Communication, 13*(1), article 14. Retrieved from http://jcmc.indiana.edu/vol13/issue1/hargittai.html.

Henderson, L. M., Zimbardo, P. G., & Carducci, B. J. (2001). Shyness. In W. E. Craighead & C. B. Nemeroff (Eds.), *The Corsini encyclopaedia of psychology and behavioral science* (pp. 1522-1523). New York; Wiley.

Joinson, A. N. (2001). Self-disclosure in computer-mediated communication: The role of self-awareness and visual anonymity. *European Journal of Social Psychology, 31*, 177-192. doi:10.1002/ejsp.36.

Kapidzic, S. (2013). Narcissism as a predictor of motivations behind Facebook profile picture selection. *Cyberpsychology, Behavior, and Social Networking, 16*, 14-19. doi:10.1089/cyber.2012.0143.

Kraut, R., Kiesler, S., Boneva, B., et al. (2002). Internet paradox revisited. *Journal of Social Issues, 58*, 49-74. doi:10.1111/1540-4560.00248.

Lee, S. Y. (2014). How do people compare themselves with others on social network sites?: The case of Facebook. *Computers in Human Behavior, 32*, 253-260. doi:10.1016 /j.chb.2013.12.009.

Leung, L. (2013). Generational differences in content generation in social media: The roles of the gratifications sought and of narcissism. *Computers in Human Behavior, 29*, 997-1006. doi:10.1016/j.chb.2012.12.028.

Levinger, G., & Rands, M. (1985). Compatibility in marriage and other close relationships. In W. Ickes (Ed.), *Compatible and incompatible relationships* (pp. 309-330). New York: Springer-Verlag.

Levinson, P. (2013). *New new media* (2nd ed.). Penguin Academics.

Ljepava, N., Orr, R. R., Locke, S., & Ross, C. (2013). Personality and social characteristics of Facebook non-users and frequent users. *Computers in Human Behavior, 29*, 1602-1607.

Lorenzen, L. A., Grieve, F. G., & Thomas, A. (2004). Exposure to muscular male models decreases men's body satisfaction. *Sex Roles, 51*(11-12), 743-748. doi:10.1007 /s11199-004-0723-0.

Machmutow, K., Perren, S., Sticca, F., & Alsaker, F. D. (2012). Peer victimization and depressive symptoms: can specific coping strategies buffer the negative impact of cyber victimization? *Emotional & Behavioral Difficulties, 17*(3/4), 403-420. doi:10.1080/ 13632752.2012.704310.

Manago, A. M., Graham, M. B., Greenfield, P. M., & Salimkhan, G. (2008). Self-presentation and gender on MySpace. *Journal of Applied Developmental Psychology, 29*(6), 446-458. doi:10.1016/j.appdev.2008.07.001.

McCroskey, J. C., & Richmond, V. P. (1990). Willingness to communicate: Different cultural perspectives. *Southern Communication Journal, 56*, 72-77. doi:10.1080 /10417949009372817.

McKenna, K. Y. A., & Bargh, J. A. (2000). Plan 9 from cyberspace: The implications of the internet for personality and social psychology. *Personality and Social Psychology Review, 4*, 57-75. doi:10.1207/S15327957PSPR0401_6.

McKinney, B. C., Kelly, L., & Duran, R. L. (2012). Narcissism or openness?: College students' use of Facebook and Twitter. *Communication Research Reports, 29*(2), 108-118. doi:10.1080/08824096.2012.666919.

Mehdizadeh, S. (2010). Self-presentation 2.0: Narcissism and self-esteem on Facebook. *Cyberpsychology, Behavior, & Social Networking, 13*, 357-364. doi:10.1089 /cyber.2009.0257.

Mendelson, A., & Papacharissi, Z. (2010). Look at us: Collective narcissism in college student Facebook photo galleries. In Z. Papacharissi (Ed.), *The networked self: Identity, community and culture on social network sites* (pp. 251-272). New York, NY: Routledge.

Menesini, E., & Nocentini, A. (2009). Cyberbullying definition and measurement: some critical considerations. *Journal of Psychology, 217,* 230–232. doi:10.1027/0044-3409.217.4.230.

Mesch, G. S. (2001). Social relationships and Internet use among adolescents in Israel. *Social Science Quarterly, 82,* 329-339. doi:10.1111/0038-4941.00026.

Morahan-Martin, J., & Schumacher, P. (2003). Loneliness and social uses of the Internet. *Computers in Human Behavior, 19,* 659-671. doi:10.1016/S0747-5632(03)00040-2.

Oltmanns, F. T., Emery, E. R., & Taylor, S. (2006). *Abnormal psychology.* Toronto: Pearson Education Canada.

Ong, E. Y. L., Ang, R. P., Ho, J. C. M., Lim, J. C. Y., Gog, D. H., Lee, C. S., et al. (2011). Narcissism, extraversion, and adolescents' self-presentation on Facebook. *Personality and Individual Differences, 50,* 180-185. doi:10.1016/j.paid.2010.09.022.

Orr, E. S., Sisic, M., Ross, C., Simmering, M. G., Arsenault, J. M., & Orr, R. R. (2009). The influence of shyness on the use of Facebook in an undergraduate sample. *CyberPsychology & Behavior, 12,* 337-340. doi:10.1089/cpb.2008.0214.

Perse, E. M., & Courtright, J. A. (1993). Normative images of communication media: Mass and interpersonal channels in the new media environment. *Human Communication Research, 19,* 485-503. doi:10.1111/j.1468-2958.1993.tb00310.x.

Peter, J., Valkenburg, P. M., & Schouten, A. P. (2005). Developing a model of adolescent friendship formation on the Internet. *CyberPsychology & Behavior, 8,* 423-430. doi:10.1089/cpb.2005.8.423.

Pittaro, M. L. (2007). Cyber stalking: An analysis of online harassment and intimidation. *International Journal of Online Harassment and Intimidation, 1,* 180-197.

Raskin, R., & Hall, C. S. (1979). A narcissistic personality inventory. *Psychological Reports, 45*(2), 590. doi:10.2466/pr0.1979.45.2.590.

Raskin, R., & Terry, H. (1988). A principal-components analysis of the narcissistic personality inventory and further evidence of its construct validity. *Journal of Personality and Social Psychology, 54*(5), 890-902.

Rosen, L. D., Cheever, N. A., & Carrier, L. M. (2012). *iDisorder: Understanding our obsession with technology and overcoming its hold on us.* New York, NY: Palgrave Macmillan.

Rosen, L. D., Whaling, K. K., Rab, S. S., Carrier, L. M., & Cheever, N. A. (2013). Is Facebook creating "iDisorders"? The link between clinical symptoms of psychiatric disorders and technology use, attitudes and anxiety. *Computers in Human Behavior, 29*(3), 1243-1254. doi:10.1016/j.chb.2012.11.012

Ross, C., Orr, E. S., Sisic, M., Arseneault, J. M., Simmering, M. G., & Orr, R. R. (2009). Personality and motivations associated with Facebook use. *Computers in Human Behavior, 25*(2), 578-586. doi: 10.1016/j.chb.2008.12.024.

Rubin, A. M., & Rubin, R. B. (1985). Interface of personal and mediated communication: A research agenda. *Critical Studies in Mass Communication, 2,* 36-53. doi:10.1080/15295038509360060.

Rutledge, C. M., Gillmor, K. L., and Gillen, M. M. (2013). Does this profile picture make me look fat? Facebook and body image in college students. *Psychology of Popular Media Culture, 2,* 251-258. doi:10.1037/ppm0000011.

Ryan, T., & Xenos, S. (2011). Who uses Facebook? An investigation into the relationship between the Big Five, shyness, loneliness, and Facebook usage. *Computers in Human Behavior, 27,* 1658-1664. doi:10.1016/j.chb.2011.02.004.

Scharlott, B. W., & Christ, W. G. (1995). Overcoming relationship-initiation barriers: The impact of a computer-dating system on sex roles, shyness, and appearance inhibitions. *Computers in Human Behavior, 11,* 191-204. doi:10.1016/0747-5632(94)00028-G.

Seidman, G. (2013). Self-presentation and belonging on Facebook: How personality influences social media use and motivations. *Personality and Individual Differences, 54,* 402-407. doi:10.1016/j.paid.2012.10.009.

Sheeks, M. S., & Birchmeier, Z. P. (2007). Shyness, sociability, and the use of computer-mediated communication in relationship development. *CyberPsychology & Behavior, 10*, 64-70. doi:10.1089/cpb.2006.9991.

Sheldon, P. (2008). The relationship between unwillingness to communicate and students' Facebook use. *Journal of Media Psychology, 20*, 67-75. doi:10.1027/1864-1105.20.2.6.

Sheldon, P. (2012). Profiling the non-users: Examination of life-position indicators, sensation seeking, shyness, and loneliness among users and non-users of social network sites. *Computers in Human Behavior, 28*, 1960-1965. doi:10.1016/j.chb.2012.05.016.

Sheldon, P. (2013a). Voices that cannot be heard: Can shyness explain how we communicate on Facebook versus face-to-face? *Computers in Human Behavior, 29*, 1402-1407. doi:10.1016/j.chb.2013.01.016.

Sheldon, P. (2013b). Testing parental and peer communication orientation influence on young adults' body satisfaction. *Southern Communication Journal, 78*(3), 215-232. doi:10.1080/1041794X.2013.776097.

Sheldon, P. (2015). *Self-monitoring and narcissism as predictors of sharing Facebook photographs.* Presented at the Southern States Communication Association conference.

Sheridan, L. P., & Grant, T. (2007). Is cyberstalking different? *Psychology, Crime, & Law, 13*, 627-640. doi:10.1080/10683160701340528.

Slonje, R., & Smith, P. K. (2008). Cyberbullying: Another main type of bullying? *Scandinavian Journal of Psychology, 49*, 147-154. doi:10.1111/j.1467-9450.2007.00611.x.

Smith, M., & Kollock, P. (1999). *Communities in cyberspace.* London: Routledge.

Sohn, S. H. (2010). Sex differences in social comparison and comparison motives in body image process. *North American Journal of Psychology, 12*, 481-500.

Spitzberg, B. H., Marshall, L., & Cupach, W. R. (2001). Obsessive relational intrusion, coping, and sexual coercion victimization. *Communication Reports, 14*, 19-30. doi:10.1080/08934210109367733.

Striegel-Moore, R., Silberstein, L. R., Frensch, P., & Rodin, J. (1989). A prospective study of disordered eating among college students. *International Journal of Eating Disorders, 8*, 499-509. doi:10.1002/1098-108X.

Stritzke, W. G. K., Nguyen, A., & Durkin, K. (2004). Shyness and computer-mediated communication: A self-presentational theory perspective. *Media Psychology, 6*, 1-22. doi:10.1207/s1532785xmep0601_1.

Thompson, J. K., Heinberg, L. J., Altabe, M., & Tantleff-Dunn, S. (1999). *Exacting beauty: Theory, assessment, and treatment of body image disturbance.* Washington, DC: American Psychological Association. doi:10.1037/10312-000.

Turkle, S. (1995). *Life on the screen: identity in the age of the Internet.* New York: Simon & Schuster.

Twenge, J. M., Konrath, S., Foster, J. D., Keith Campbell, W. W., & Bushman, B. J. (2008). Egos inflating over time: A cross-temporal meta-analysis of the Narcissistic Personality Inventory. *Journal of Personality, 76*(4), 875-902. doi:10.1111/j.1467-6494.2008.00507.x.

Uhls, Y. T., and Greenfield, P. M. (2012). The value of fame: Preadolescent perceptions of popular media and their relationship to future aspirations. *Developmental Psychology, 48*(2), 315-326. doi:10.1037/a0026369.

Utz, S. (2010). Show me your friends and I will tell you what type of a person you are: How one's profile, number of friends, and type of friends influence impression formation on social network sites. *Journal of Computer-Mediated Communication, 15*, 314-335. doi:10.1111/j.1083-6101.2010.01522.x.

Utz, S., Tanis, M., & Vermeulen, I. (2012). It's all about being popular: The effects of need for popularity on social network site use. *Cyberpsychology, Behavior, and Social Networking, 15*, 37-42. doi:10.1089/cyber.2010.0651.

Valkenburg, P. M., & Peter, J. (2007). Adolescents online communication and their well-being: Testing the simulation versus the displacement hypothesis. *Journal of Computer-Mediated Communication, 12*(4), article 2.

Vandoninck, S., d'Haenens, L., De Cock, R., & Donoso, V. (2012). Social networking sites and contact risks among Flemish youth. *Childhood, 19*(1), 69-85. doi:10.1177 /0907568211406456.

Walther, J. B. (1992). Interpersonal effects in computer-mediated interaction: a relational perspective. *Communication Research, 19,* 52-90. doi:10.1177 /009365092019001003.

Walther, J. B. (1996). Computer-mediated communication: Impersonal, interpersonal, and hyperpersonal interaction. *Communication Research, 23,* 3-43. doi:10.1177 /009365096023001001.

Walther, J. B. (2007). Selective self-presentation in computer-mediated communication: Hyperpersonal dimensions of technology language, and cognition. *Computers in Human Behavior, 23,* 2538-2557. doi:10.1016/j.chb.2006.05.002.

Ward, C. C., & Tracey, T. J. G. (2004). Relation of shyness with aspects of online relationship involvement. *Journal of Social and Personal Relationships, 21,* 611-623. doi:10.1177/0265407504045890.

Weiss, R. S. (Ed.). (1973). *Loneliness: The experience of emotional and social isolation.* Cambridge, MA: MIT Press.

Welsh, A. & Lavoie, J. A. A. (2012). Risky eBusiness: An examination of risk-taking, online disclosiveness, and cyberstalking victimization. *Cyberpsychology: Journal of Psychosocial Research on Cyberspace, 6*(1), article 4. doi:10.5817/CP2012-1-4.

Winter, S., Neubaum, G., Eimler, S. C., Gordon, V., Theil, J., Herrmann, J., Meinert, J., & Krämer, N. C. (2014). Another brick in the Facebook wall—How personality traits relate to the content of status updates. *Computers in Human Behavior, 34,* 194-202. doi:10.1016/j.chb.2014.01.048.

Zhao, S., Grasmuck, S., & Martin, J. (2008). Identity construction on Facebook: Digital empowerment in anchored relationships. *Computers in Human Behavior, 24,* 1816-36. doi:10.1016/j.chb.2008.02.012.

II

Applications of Social Media

FOUR

Social Media in Politics

The Internet and social media are changing the way that we communicate, organize, and socialize. Political campaigning on the Internet began in 1996 when a number of candidates created their own websites. It was not until 2004 that citizens took advantage of new information communication technology to gain knowledge of the candidates. Howard Dean, a Democratic presidential candidate, pioneered new ways of engaging supporters online by raising $40 million for his campaign over the course of the primaries. Dean was the first candidate with his own blog. In 2008, the Obama campaign surpassed Dean by using social media to mobilize supporters, especially young voters who were already on MySpace, Facebook, and Twitter. On Facebook alone, over 1,000 groups were created for each of the two major political party candidates (Barack Obama and John McCain, year 2008). Social media with political relevance include: blogs (HuffingtonPost), microblogs (Twitter, Google Buzz), social networking (Facebook), professional networks (LinkedIn), video (YouTube, Vimeo), and livestreaming (Livestream, Justin.tv).

BLOGS AND HOWARD DEAN

Blogs played a significant part in the 2004 U.S. presidential elections. Political blogs were linked to other blogs with similar ideologies, but they discussed the same issues as traditional media during the election season (Lee, 2007). One of the reasons was limited resources for gathering information, and, therefore, heavy dependence on reports from traditional media (Lee, 2007). Professional journalists also created their own personal blogs during the 2004 elections, and news organizations (*New York Times, New Republic, ABC*) hosted their own blogs (Lawson-Borders & Kirk, 2005). The growing popularity of blogs at this time was evidenced

57

by the fact that Merriam-Webster's dictionary rated the word "blog" as the #1 Word of the Year for 2004. Unlike traditional media that are more hierarchical and limited, blogs have appeal because they allow participants to express themselves more freely. They are available 24 hours a day, and people from all over the country and the world can engage in a political discussion (Mattheson, 2004). Mattheson wrote: "The line between journalism and other forms is blurred by the many news-related weblogs maintained by people who are not employed as journalists" (p. 449).

The first effective use of blogs as an organizing and motivating tool started with Howard Dean, a former Vermont governor. With the help of the Dean Weblog, a social network, Meetup.com, and hundreds of bloggers, he entered the race for the Democratic Party's presidential nomination. Meetup.com was founded by Scott Heiferman in 2002 to make it easy for people with similar interests to find each other and arrange face-to-face meetings (Sifry, 2011). At the time, the site was considered an e2f (electronic-to-face) community which allows citizens to find each other and organize online so that they can get together offline (Weinberg & Williams, 2006). The premise of Meetup.com was "set a date, time, and place for like-minded strangers to gather" (Gray, 2004).

Dean said that a lot of people had given up on traditional politics precisely because "they had no way to shout back." Traditional media did not allow for a two-way communication. It was not until the New York City Dean Meetup in early 2003 that Dean realized how many supporters were waiting in line to see him. People who had been to at least one Dean Meetup reported giving $154 on average to his campaign (Sifry, 2011). Dean broke the record for money raised by any Democratic candidate before him. In a study of 820 people who attended meet-ups for presidential candidates between January and March 2004, attendance was found to be positively related to campaign effectiveness including donations, volunteering, candidate support and advocacy (Weinberg & Williams, 2006).

What was the secret of Howard Dean? Dean and his campaign manager, Joe Tripolli, let things happen from the bottom up. A decentralized network of supporters was playing the most important role. His local and national volunteer infrastructure arose with little help or supervision (Wolf, 2004). Journalist Gary Wolf (2004) cites the physicist Albert-Laszlo Barabasi, who argued that "popularity breeds more popularity." In other words, links are posted on websites that have the most links. That is the idea of democracy: "People talking with each other about what matters to them" (David Weinberger, as cited in Wolf, 2004). Dean's campaign was a "stupid network," according to Wolf (2004). A stupid network is one that is not optimized for any set of definitive uses. Instead, the network is simple and requires very little direction from headquarters. For instance, Meetup.com supporters organized themselves and held monthly meetings across the country. The majority of meet-ups were middle-age, middle-income professionals interested in politics. Dean's campaign also organized a "Generation Dean" website, aimed at attracting younger voters.

Although Howard Dean did not win the primary elections, in less than one year he went from being politically unknown to a front-runner, appearing on the cover of *Time* magazine in 2003 (Weinberg & Williams, 2006). Weinberg and Williams argued that Dean's innovative use of the Internet for political purposes is comparable to John F. Kennedy's use of network television during the 1960 campaign against Richard Nixon, and with Bill Clinton's use of cable television in the 1992 campaign against George H. W. Bush. Ron Paul in 2011 had about 88,000 supporters on Meetup.com, and some argue that the Tea Party was born on the site. However, this site might not be working for every candidate. In a 2004 article, Carol Darr, director of George Washington University's Institute for Politics, Democracy and the Internet, warned that the site requires a charismatic president or a charismatic idea to get people to plug in (Gray, 2004).

While Howard Dean succeeded in using the web to generate early support, he did not win in 2004. Four years later, Obama did. In 2008, young voters tuned into social network sites like Facebook and Twitter to receive campaign news. They turned out to the polls in the highest numbers since 1972. A record-breaking 46 percent of Americans used the Internet, e-mail, or cell phone text messaging to get news about the 2008 campaign, share their views, and mobilize others (Pew Charitable Trust, 2008).

SOCIAL MEDIA IN THE 2008 AND 2012 CAMPAIGNS

Although blogs were not fully utilized in the 2004 campaign—and did not influence the outcome of the election—they provided an example for how citizen journalists can contribute to political organizing (Lawson-Borders & Kirk, 2005). Social network sites like Facebook and Twitter played a much more important role in the 2008 elections.

Obama's campaign hired Facebook co-founder Chris Hughes to create the myBarackObama.com network. The site offered a blog, detailed supporter profiles, personalized fundraising pages, videos, speeches, and photos, as well as event-planning tools. By the end of the campaign, it had 2 million active users. Overall, Obama's team used fifteen online social networks to sell his message. In 2008, the Obama-Biden campaign reached 5 million supporters on social networks. When compared to his runner-up, John McCain, Obama's team used the Internet more efficiently, creating more Facebook groups and attracting more young people (Woolley, Limperos, & Oliver, 2010). Social network sites helped in mobilization efforts as people watched candidate debates and speeches via YouTube. The best example is the Obama Girl video, named a top ten meme of the decade by Newsweek. Amber Lee Ettinger appeared in the "I got a crush on Obama" viral video, posted on YouTube in June 2007. The video features a young woman singing of her love for then-U.S. Senator Obama. The video was not sponsored by the Obama campaign— but it reached millions of viewers, contributing to Obama's popularity. Over the course of the 2008 election cycle, both young adults and senior citizens were highly involved in political campaigning. In fact, those who used Facebook were five times more likely to vote, to attend rallies or meetings, and to try to convince their friends to vote (Hampton, Goulet, Rainie, & Purcell, 2011). By the end of the campaign, Obama had raised more than $500 million online from three million donors with an average online donation of $80. Obama's team collected 13 million e-mail addresses and sent more than 7,000 messages (Levenshus, 2010).

Obama continued his presence on social media in 2012, reaching 27.6 million Facebook friends, 207,000 YouTube subscribers, and over 18 million Twitter followers. Compared to Mitt Romney, his campaign posted nearly four times as much content (Pew Research Journalism Project, 2012a). The greatest gap was on Twitter, with Obama posting 29 tweets and Romney averaging one tweet per day. Obama's campaign also had twice as many public accounts on social media as did Romney's campaign. However, every post on Facebook and YouTube came directly from the campaign (Pew Research Journalism Project, 2012a). Neither candidate focused on the social aspects of social media, such as replying to or commenting on something from a citizen.

The range of issues on Obama's website substantially narrowed in 2012 when compared to 2008. Compared to Obama, Romney's campaign focused on many more issues. The two candidates also employed different messaging strategies. According to the Pew Research Journalism Project (2012b), Romney relied on visuals, graphics, photos, and videos, while Obama used more text. While both candidates' focus was mostly on domestic policy, Obama's second biggest focus was fundraising and volunteering, and Romney's was campaign activities. Although the economy was the No. 1 issue for both campaigns in their digital messaging, the economy was not what voters showed the most interest in. On average, Obama's messages about the economy generated 361 shares per post, while his posts about immigration generated more than four times that reaction (Pew Research Journalism Project, 2012a).

Obama's campaign managers integrated the Internet into their grassroots strategy. E-mails that were sent to people, as well as the MyBO website, encouraged supporters to organize events and meet face-to-face (Levenshus, 2010). The site also included language such as "Take action now," emphasizing the action, but also being personalized and you-centered. According to Obama's campaign staff member Mitch Stewart (personal communication, December 4, 2008; as cited in Levenshus, 2010), the Internet and website served as a feeder system into the campaign, attracting the volunteers and future supporters. Anyone who signed up online was involved in person.

Obama's use of social media, however, was not a novelty in media history. Franklin Roosevelt used radio for his Fireside Chats, and John F. Kennedy embraced television However, Barack Obama might have become president because of social media. In his book *New New Media*, Paul Levinson (2013) argues that Obama's victory was facilitated by social media.

DO SOCIAL MEDIA IMPACT POLITICAL CAMPAIGNS?

The advantages of using social media in political campaigns include the following:

- Access to politically relevant information
- A shift from the uni-directional flow of information toward peer-to-peer (P2P) sharing (Jenkins, 2006)
- The so-called "tell-a-friend" feature that enables people to forward the campaign message to their friends
- A better cost-benefit ratio: a YouTube video is free; a TV ad costs millions
- Quick results with little investment of time and effort
- A level of intimacy as people share posts with friends and family; on television a candidate appears distant
- Less intrusion compared to e-mails

Takaragawa and Carty (2012) discuss the "tell-a-friend" phenomenon that alters how individuals receive information. For example, a video forwarded from a friend through social media is more enthusiastically received than a television advertisement, as people trust those whom they already know, or with whom they share a personal connection. In another study, researchers (Noort, Antheunis, & van Reijmersdal, 2012) found that social network users who receive a marketing campaign from a strong social connection (such as family and friends) hold a more positive attitude toward the campaign, and were more inclined to forward it to their own connections. Another advantage of social media is targeted political campaigns (Christopoulos, 2013). Because it is possible to purchase sociodemographic information about those using social media, it is therefore possible to sell ideas the same way that products are sold. Voter segmentation can thus be highly sophisticated (Christopoulos, 2013). For example, in 2012 the Obama campaign tailored its message to 26 different voter segments. Other scholars (Bekafigo, Cohen, Gainous, & Wagner, 2013) argued that while social media were not intended to be political portals, they have been adapted to that purpose. President Obama and members of Congress are using Twitter to send short statements to their supporters. The Internet and social media have become a vital element of a national campaign including communication, campaigning, fundraising, and organization (Gainous & Wagner, 2011). In addition, social media tools allow nontraditional candidates to compete for public office where they would otherwise be disadvantaged (Allison, 2002; Wagner & Gainous, 2009). Equalization theory (Barber, 2001) argues that the Internet is a positive democratizing entity that helps remove the barriers that favor some groups and parties in the electorate.

LaMarre and Suzuki-Lambrecht (2013) examined the effectiveness of Twitter as a public relations communications tool for the 2010 congressional campaigns. Their results revealed that congressional campaigns that used Twitter, were more likely to win their elections than those who did not use Twitter. They also found that the number of tweets sent by a candidate did not help them win the elections; rather, the number of followers a candidate had significantly increased their odds of winning. LaMarre and Suzuki-Lambrecht concluded that the key to Twitter's effectiveness lies in developing a large and engaged audience. Similarly, Levenshus (2010) examined the Obama-Biden campaign's effectiveness in engaging citizens through social media during the 2008 presidential election. They found that the grassroots activism strategies were successfully implemented through social media, resulting in increased commitment to the candidate. Ifukor (2010) reported the results of an analysis of 245 blog posts and 923 Tweets surrounding the 2007 Nigerian electoral cycle. The results showed that Twitter was an alternative avenue of participatory politics. Jungherr (2014) analyzed Twitter messages commenting on politics during the campaign for the 2009 federal election in Germany. The study revealed that the content of Twitter messages follows a hybrid logic of political coverage. Sometimes, it follows the same logic as the coverage of political actors in the traditional news media, and, at other times, it is following the logic of social media. Jungherr (2014) cites Andrew Chadwick who calls this phenomenon "the hybrid media system" (Chadwick, 2013). Chadwick argued that political communication in both traditional and social media are interconnected and mutually dependent. However, the events covered on Twitter are reported differently than in traditional media, according to Papacharissi and de Fatima Oliveira (2012). According to them, the news on Twitter are based on subjective experiences, opinions, and emotions. Jungherr (2014) found that Twitter messages also showed evidence of new uses. This included the mobilization of nontraditional parties, as well as high levels of ironic commentary. In other cases, the content of messages also followed the logic of traditional media: personalization, contest, horserace coverage, and indexing (Jungherr, 2014).

DISADVANTAGES OF USING SOCIAL MEDIA

While television was a community medium that people of all political spectrums watched, in the digital age, the Internet provides media consumers with a choice to select which news items they wish to read. As a result, people interact with individuals who have the same ideology (Warner & Neville-Shepard, 2011). Warner and Neville-Shepard argued that digital media contribute to fragmentation and polarization among the media audience. According to them, "this 'opt in/opt out' version of politics is necessarily more polarized because many passive and moderate voices have exited the conversation" (p. 202). Warner and Neville-Shepard's analysis of archived blogs from Dean's blogforamerica.com website indicated antagonistic themes such as "take back our country." They also found common references to the American Revolution and noted that Dean's campaign attacked traditional media, accusing them of "keeping politics an elite-dominated event" (p. 208). Some other researchers (e.g., Sunstein, 2007) also cited Dean's blog as an example of antagonism, arguing that such fragmentation will lead to polarization and possible extremism, hatred, and violence. However, unlike the Dean blogs, Obama blogs did not focus on the antagonistic elements. For the bloggers supporting Obama, McCain was not an enemy, but "merely a less desirable candidate" (p. 211).

FACEBOOK POLITICAL GROUPS

Politics have always been about networking. Politicians are thus using Facebook, Twitter, and YouTube to reach segmented communities and narrowcast messages to party members in specific districts, at particular times of the day, and for specific purposes (Elmer & Langlois, 2013). However, there are some limitations to Facebook political groups. The first one is the false consensus effect (Woolley et al., 2010). It is the idea that most of the people in the population share the same point of view (Marks & Miller, 1987). In addition, studies have suggested that overall the information content and quality of discussion on the walls of Facebook political groups was very low (Conroy, Feezell, & Guerrero, 2012). Moreover, the views expressed in those groups might reflect similar topics as those featured in other media venues (Woolley et al., 2010). Similarly, when conducting content analyses of blog posts and mainstream media news stories during the 2004 presidential campaign, Lee (2007) found that the blog agenda was similar to that of mainstream media.

Social media and new technologies have become a popular public relations tool for many governments (Hong, 2013), becoming "a central component of e-government" (Bertot, Jaeger, & Hansen, 2012). New technologies have changed the way government communicates with its citizens. Previous research has shown that a high-quality government web-site can foster credibility of both the website and the government, allow-ing government transparency—the easier access to information regarding government policies and activities (Searson & Johnson, 2010; as cited in Hong, 2013). This has led to a higher public trust in government, which many see as a central foundation of democracy (Sadeghi, 2012). Accord-ing to the 2011 e-government survey (Norris & Reddick, 2011), most local governments in the United States use at least one social medium. The most popular channels include Facebook, then Twitter, and YouTube. Hong (2013) analyzed data of more than 2,000 American citizens to find out whether individuals' experience with government websites and so-cial media influence their perception of the government-public relation-ship. Hong found that the respondents' experience with social media had a positive effect on their trust in government at the local and state level. Those who interacted with their local government through social media were more likely to trust their government. However, this was not really the case with the federal government websites. As Hong (2013) and other scholars (Schario & Konisky, 2008) suggested, citizens often trust local governments more because they have a direct experience with them, while national newscasts often focus on unpleasant performances of the federal government. Finally, despite the idea of a two-way communica-tion between the government and the public, research (Norris & Reddick, 2013; Waters & Williams, 2011) suggests that the current government applications remain mainly as a one-way communication.

When it comes to the government-citizen relationship, Linders (2012) argued that social media offer a number of advantages over its offline variants, including the fact that is much easier to attract members with similar interests, exchange information, as well as supervise and manage groups with less need for hierarchy. Citizen coproduction, Linders (2012) and Johnston and Hansen (2011) argued, has become more relevant with the advances in technology. Three types of co-production exist today (Linders, 2012): "citizen to government," "government to citizen," and "citizen to citizen" types. "Citizen to government" category includes government consulting with the public through social media channels such as Facebook and Twitter. An example is President Obama's change.gov initiative. This category includes service monitoring and citi-zen reporting (Linders, 2012). Citizens can efficiently and conveniently share knowledge with the government. For instance, they can take photos of criminal fugitives or natural disaster damage and send it to the authorities for action. Another category is "government to citizen" or "government as a platform idea." Linders (2012) mentioned the govern-ment delivering highly personalized information to help citizens make a decision. That can include health risks information, useful government programs to apply for, and neighborhood crime. Finally, the third catego-ry includes "citizen to citizen" or "do-it-yourself government." Social media can help citizens to more effectively self-organize. That can include direct citizen-to-citizen assistance but also coordinating actions when government fails (Linders, 2012). The Arab Spring movement is a recent example. Proponents of coproduction have argued that it helps foster social capital, strengthen civil society (Torres, 2007), promote innovation, and engage the poor and disadvantaged (Bovaird, 2007) who otherwise would not have participated.

SOCIAL MEDIA IN THE ARAB SPRING

Many people have argued that social media acted as a powerful "accelerating agent" facilitating the overturn of authoritarian regimes in the Arab world (Frangonikolopoulos & Chapsos, 2012; Zhuo, Wellmann, & Yu, 2011). The 2010 Arab Spring movement started in Tunisia and then spread to other Middle Eastern and North African countries. While traditional media are tightly restricted and controlled in authoritarian regimes, social media in the Arab world were seen as a free, unrestricted media to share disagreements with the government. When the Iranian president Mahmoud Ahmadinejad won the presidential election in 2009, the so-called "Green Revolution" started using social media to document the struggle of protesters (Ali & Fahmy 2013). Twitter was the most popular medium during the protests, which led many to suggest that the 2009 post-Iranian election was the birth of *citizen journalists* (Human Rights Watch, Iran, 2010; as cited in Ali & Fahmy, 2013). Especially popular was the YouTube video showing the murder of Neda Agha-Soltan, a philosophy student who was a bystander to the protests when she was shot in the chest on Kargar Street in Tehran.

On seeing what was happening in Iran and frustrated with the authoritarian regime and poverty—activists in Egypt and Libya began calling on the public to protest against the 30-year-old regime of President Mubarak (Ali & Fahmy, 2013). In January of 2011, the so-called "Facebook Revolution" started in Egypt. Zhuo et al. (2011) argued that social media helped transform Egyptian society. While only 29 percent of people had Internet access in Egypt in 2010, a "Facebook Generation" of educated males decided to reject the traditionalism, the hierarchy, and the social and economic insecurity. The movement is often described as the "Triple Revolution" (Zhuo et al., 2011), including:

1. The turn to social networks
2. The proliferation of the instantaneous Internet
3. Always-available mobile phones

Young people in the Arab world used social networks even before the revolution. Mobile phones are cheap and easy to conceal while taking photos of protests. Photos can also be shared via cell phones. However, while activists used the Internet to spread the word and form linkages with the Progressive Youth of Tunisia movement, they still had to rely on an informal network consisting of people who did not have Internet access. Many people also learned about protests through face-to-face communication or word of mouth. Others used text messages to share the images with the public. Zhou et al. (2011) used the term "networked individualism" when describing a networked society with less group control and more autonomy.

Social media also had another important role in the Arab Spring movement. They helped build a sense of community and minimize the feeling of isolation. The best example is the creation of a Facebook page and a YouTube video, "We are all Khaled Said." Khaled Said (Saeed) was a young Egyptian man whom police beat to death while sitting in a cyber café at night. Said was killed for posting video footage of police corruption (Ali & Fahmy, 2013). The killing outraged civil activists. Wael Ghonim, a Google executive for the Middle East and North Africa, created this page. The Facebook page attracted thousands of fans, and the international community pressured the Egyptian government to try two police officers involved in his death. The page became one of the many catalysts for other protests throughout Egypt. A YouTube video of Khaled Said was also created, showing contrasting images of Said happy with graphic images from the morgue (Preston, 2011). Khaled Said was not much different from other protesters who were killed in Egypt; however, his life became known due to the social media that spread his story (Halverson, Ruston, & Trethewey, 2013). Halverson et al. argued that images of Kahled Said on the "We are all Khaled Said" Facebook page serve as visual manifestations of the martyr.

According to Hall (2012), the number of Facebook users in Egypt rose from 450,000 to 3 million in the six months following the revolution. Facebook was used primarily to raise awareness about the ongoing uprising (31 percent), organize activists and actions (30 percent), and spread information to the world about it (24 percent). Only 15 percent of the users used it for entertainment (Salem & Mourtada, 2011). Encouraged by the events in Iran and Egypt, in February 2011 Libyans started protesting President Gaddafi's government. As soon as the protests began, Gaddafi blocked all communication including television and Internet. However, Libyan citizens still used their own cameras to document the chaos. Twitter became an important tool in helping end the Gaddafi regime. Gaddafi was killed in October 2011.

ARE SOCIAL MEDIA RESPONSIBLE FOR
THE ARAB SPRING?

After a long debate, scholars seem to agree that social media played a soft deterministic role in the Arab Spring. Hirst argued (2012) that we have to be careful when linking the protests to social media determinism. Journalism is only "the first draft" of history. He warns that the events in Tunisia, Bahrain, Egypt, Yemen, Libya, and Syria, including the democracy movement and the workers' movement, started long before January 2011. "It was the old-fashioned working class that enabled the pro-democracy movement to flourish" (Lee & Weinthall, 2012, p. 283). Hirst (2012) argued that Western journalists just did not know much about the happenings in the Arab World and were not prepared for the events, so when the protests happened, they were feeding off online citizen journalism. He argued that this type of bias, a "bias of convenience" (the term coined by the Princeton historian Edward Tenner), creates a certain level of groupthink and pack mentality among reporters (also Tiffen, 1989). Hirst (2012) argued that the bias of convenience and soft determinism are still present in popular journalism, and that might be the reason that social media are seen as a necessary catalyst in the Arab Spring movement. In other words, citizen journalists acted as correspondents for global media.

McCafferty (2011) explained the Arab Spring movement in terms of activism versus slacktivism. Slacktivism refers to people who are happy to click a "like" button about a cause, but they are not inspired by it. An example is an online letter-writing campaign where supporters copy-paste from a template form of the letter and are not asked to come up with their own words. McCafferty argues that that is not activism and emphasizes the difference between traditional movements and a modern ones. Traditional movements are organized around strong personal ties (church members, classmates). On the other hand, activism through social media relies on weak ties. McCafferty concludes that the Arab Spring demonstrations just used social media to broadcast what was happening. Activism, however, was and will always be about the people. Gladwell (2010) also noted that weak ties do not lead to high-risk activism. He offered the American civil rights movement as an example. It happened because of strong ties or strong personal connections.

Ali and Fahmy (2013) shared similar views. According to them, social media was not the sole cause of the revolutions in Iran, Libya, and Egypt. They made it logistically easier, but word of mouth was the main medium activists used. They argued that traditional media continued to maintain hegemony by being the major source of information for citizens during the Arab Spring. An example is the Facebook page for Khaled Said that became popular only after its creator appeared on Dream TV, and Al-Jazeera picked up coverage of Said. Although the Egyptian revolution was known as the "Facebook Revolution," Ali and Fahmy argued that social networking sites were just another tool that citizens used to warn the international media about the crisis at home. In Iran, Egypt, and Libya, the most powerful tools for the spread of information was word of mouth (Ali & Fahmy, 2013). Social media, however, united people during the revolutions. Social media were a facilitator of the revolutions (Halverson et al., 2013).

In his early work, communication scholar and technological determinist[1] Marshall McLuhan (*Understanding Media*, 1964) argued that all technology is communication, and the medium is the message. He believed that the form dominates the content. McLuhan saw communication technologies as the engine of social change (Carey, 1967). Unlike hard determinism in which A is all that is necessary to cause B (pouring a water over your head is all that is necessary to make your head wet), in soft determinism, there might be other things necessary for the condition to happen (Levinson, 2013). In the context of the Arab Spring, social media were not responsible for the uprising, but they accelerated it. The creator of the "We are all Khaled Said" Facebook page, Wael Ghomin, compared the Revolution 2.0 in Egypt to a Wikipedia site where everybody contributes small pieces, but there is no one leader. Everybody is a citizen journalist. Ali and Fahmy (2013) further examined the characteristics of gatekeeping practices by citizen journalists. White (1950) defined gatekeeping as a selection process where gatekeepers pick and choose which news articles they are going to run in the media. Ali and Fahmy argued that user-generated content does not threaten traditional media, and, in fact, is subjected to the same gatekeeping rules propagated by professional journalists. In fact, traditional media has picked up information from social media that they considered newsworthy, mostly focusing on human-interest stories.

Social media played an important role in connecting the entire Arab world in their common struggle for democracy and change (Frangonikolopoulos & Chapsos, 2012). Social media allowed ordinary citizens to express their disagreement with the governments, to spread information, raise awareness of civil society, disseminate courage, and provide support. Beckett (2011) argued that social media gave people a sense of solidarity and the permission to go further. It united them and it empowered them toward one goal. Ultimately, the whole world was watching.

Lindsey (2013) argued that "in Syria, social media offer a medium for obtaining international sympathy and support for a cause." Amateur clips sent via cell phone or posted on Facebook and YouTube helped the world to see what Basher al-Assad's regime was doing to its civilians. However, in 2013, Lindsey acknowledged the fact that many people in the Middle East are still not using social media, and 70 percent still rely on television programs for information.

NOTE

1. The term "technological determinism" was coined by Thornstein Veblen (1857–1929), an American sociologist who presumed that technology drives the development of the society and its culture.

REFERENCES

Ali, S. R., & Fahmy, S. (2013). Gatekeeping and citizen journalism: The use of social media during the recent uprisings in Iran, Egypt, and Libya. *Media, War, & Conflict, 6*(1), 55-69. doi:10.1177/1750635212469906.

Allison, J. E. (2002). *Technology, development, and democracy: International conflict and cooperation in the information age, SUNY series in global politics.* Albany: State University of New York Press.

Barber, B. R. (2001). The uncertainty of digital politics. *Harvard International Review, 23*(1), 42-47.

Beckett, T. (2011). *After Tunisia and Egypt: Towards a new typology of media and networked political change.* Retrieved from http://blogs.lse.ac.uk/polis/2011/02/11/after-tunisia -and-egypt-towards-a-new-typology-of-media-and-networked-political-change/.

Bekafigo, M., Cohen, D., Gainous, J., & Wagner, K. (2013). State parties 2.0: Facebook, campaigns, and elections. *The International Journal of Technology, Knowledge, and Society, 9,* 99-112.

Bertot, J. C., Jaeger, P. T., & Hansen, D. (2012). The impact of policies on government social media usage: Issues, challenges, and recommendations. *Government Information Quarterly, 29,* 30–40.

Bovaird, T. (2007). Beyond engagement and participation: User and community co-production of public services. *Public Administration Review, 67*(5), 846–860.

Carey, J. W. (1967). Harold Adams Innis and Marshall McLuhan. *The Antioch Review, 27*(1), 5-39. doi:10.2307/4610816.

Chadwick, A. (2013). *The hybrid media system: Politics and power.* Oxford, England: Oxford University Press.

Christopoulos, D. (2013, July). *Does social media impact political campaigns? Volatility and salience in political discourse.* Presented at the NCSL Symposium for Legislative Leaders, Scottish Parliament.

Conroy, M., Feezell, J., & Guerrero, M. (2012). Facebook and political engagement: A study of online political group membership and offline political engagement. *Computers in Human Behavior, 28*(5), 1535-1546. doi:10.1016/j.chb.2012.03.012.

Elmer, G., & Langlois, G. (2013). Networked campaigns: Traffic tags and cross platform analysis on the web. *Information Polity, 18*(1), 43-56. doi:10.3233/IP-2011-244.

Frangonikolopoulos, C., & Chapsos, I. (2012). Explaining the role and impact of the social media in the Arab Spring. *GMJ: Mediterranean Edition, 8*(1), 10-20.

Gainous, J., & Wagner, K. (2011). *Rebooting American politics: The Internet revolution.* Lanham, MD: Rowman and Littlefield.

Gladwell, M. (2010, October 4). Small change: Why the revolution will not be tweeted. *The New Yorker.* Retrieved from http://www.newyorker.com/reporting/2010/10/04 /101004fa_fact_gladwell?currentPage=all.

Gray, C. (2004, February 11). Meetup.com working to become a force in local, state politics. *Knight Ridder Tribune.* Retrieved from http://www.highbeam.com/doc/1G1 -113163315.html.

Hall, E. (2012). Year after Arab Spring, digital, social media shape region's rebirth. *Advertising Age, 83*(24), 10.

Halverson, J. R., Ruston, S. W., & Trethewey, A. (2013). Mediated martyrs of the Arab Spring: New media, civil religion, and narrative in Tunisia and Egypt. *Journal of Communication, 63*(2), 312-332. doi:10.1111/jcom.12017.

Hampton, K., Goulet, L. S., Rainie, L., & Purcell, K. (2011). *Social networking sites and our lives*. Retrieved from http://www.pewinternet.org/2011/06/16/social-networking-sites-and-our-lives/.

Hirst, M. (2012). One tweet does not a revolution make: Technological determinism, media and social change. *Global Media Journal*, *12*, 1-29.

Hong, H. (2013). Government websites and social media's influence on government-public relationships. *Public Relations Review*, *39*, 346-356. doi:10.1016/j.pubrev.2013.07.007.

Human Rights Watch (2010) Iran. Retrieved from http://www.hrw.org/en/node/87713.

Ifukor, P. (2010). "Elections" or "selections"? Blogging and twittering the Nigerian 2007 general elections. *Bulletin of Science, Technology & Society*, *30*(6), 398-414. doi:10.1177/0270467610380008.

Jenkins, H. (2006). *Convergence culture*. New York: New York University Press.

Johnston, E., & Hansen, D. (2011). Design lessons for smart governance infrastructures. In D. Ink, A. Balutis, and T. Buss (Eds.), *American governance 3.0: Rebooting the public square?* (pp. 197-212). National Academy of Public Administration.

Jungherr, A. (2014). The logic of political coverage on Twitter: Temporal dynamics and content. *Journal of Communication*, *64*, 239-259. doi:10.1111/jcom.12087.

LaMarre, H. L., & Suzuki-Lambrecht, Y. (2013). Tweeting democracy? Examining Twitter as an online public relations strategy for congressional campaigns. *Public Relations Review*, *39*(4), 360-368. doi:10.1016/j.pubrev.2013.07.009.

Lawson-Borders, G., & Kirk, R. (2005). Blogs in campaign communication. *American Behavioral Scientist*, *49*, 548-559. doi:10.1177/0002764205279425.

Lee, E., & Weinthall, B. (2012). The truly revolutionary social networks. In T. Manhire (Ed.), *The Arab Spring: Rebellion, revolution and a new world order* (pp. 283-285). London: Guardian Books.

Lee, J. K. (2007). The effect of the Internet on homogeneity of the media agenda: A test of the fragmentation thesis. *Journalism & Mass Communication Quarterly*, *84*, 745-760. doi: 10.1177/107769900708400406.

Levenshus, A. (2010). Online relationship management in a presidential campaign: A case study of the Obama campaign's management of its Internet-integrated grass-roots effort. *Journal of Public Relations Research*, *22*(3), 313-335. doi:10.1080/10627261003614419.

Levinson, P. (2013). *New new media*. Pearson/Penguin Academics.

Linders, D. (2012). From e-government to we-government: Defining a typology for citizen coproduction in the age of social media. *Government Information Quarterly*, *29*, 446-454. doi:10.1016/j.giq.2012.06.003.

Lindsey, R. (2013). What the Arab Spring tells us about the future of social media in revolutionary movements. *Small Wars Journal*, *9*(7). Retrieved from http://small-warsjournal.com/jrnl/art/what-the-arab-spring-tells-us-about-the-future-of-social-media-in-revolutionary-movements.

Marks, G., & Miller, N. (1987). Ten years of research on the false-consensus effect: An empirical and theoretical review. *Psychological Bulletin*, *102*(1), 72-90. doi:10.1037/0033-2909.102.1.72.

Mattheson, D. (2004).Weblogs and the epistemology of the news: Some trends in online journalism. *New Media & Society*, *6*, 443-468. doi:10.1177/146144804044329.

McCafferty, D. (2011). Activism vs. slacktivism. *Communications of the ACM*, *54*(12), 17-19. doi:10.1145/2043174.2043182.

McLuhan, M. (1964). *Understanding media: The extension of man*. London: Sphere Books.

(van) Noort, G., Antheunis, M., & van Reijmersdal, E. (2012). Social connections and the persuasiveness of viral campaigns in social network sites: Persuasive intent as the underlying mechanism. *Journal of Marketing Communications*, *18*(1), 39-53. doi:10.1080/13527266.2011.620764.

Norris, D. F., & Reddick, C. G. (2011). *E-government 2011 survey*. Retrieved from http://icma.org/en/icma/knowledge network/documents/kn/Document/302947/.

Norris, D. F., & Reddick, C. G. (2013). Local e-government in the United States: Transformation or incremental change? *Public Administration Review, 73*(1), 165–175. doi:10.1111/j.1540-6210.2012.02647.x.

Papacharissi, Z., & de Fatima Oliveira, M. (2012). Affective news and networked publics: The rhythms of news storytelling on #Egypt. *Journal of Communication, 62,* 266-282. doi:10.1111/j.1460-2466.2012.01630.x.

Pew Charitable Trust (2008). *A record-breaking 46 percent of Americans have already used Internet for politics this election season.* Retrieved from http://www.pewtrusts.org/en /about/news-room/press-releases/2008/06/15/a-recordbreaking-46-of-americans -have-already-used-internet-for-politics-this-election-season.

Pew Research Journalism Project (2012a, August 15). *How the presidential candidates use the web and social media.* Retrieved from http://www.journalism.org/2012/08/15/how -presidential-candidates-use-web-and-social-media/.

Pew Research Journalism Project (2012b, August 15). *Messaging – two different strategies.* Retrieved from http://www.journalism.org/2012/08/15/messaging-two -different-strategies/.

Preston, J. (2011, February 5). Movement began with outrage and a Facebook page that gave it an outlet. *New York Times.* Retrieved from http://www.nytimes.com/2011/02 /06/world/middleeast/06face.html?pagewanted=all&_r=0.

Sadeghi, L. (2012). Web 2.0. In M. Lee, G. Neeley, & K. Stewart (Eds.), *The practice of government public relations* (pp. 25–140). Boca Raton, FL: CRC Press.

Salem, F., & Mourtada, R. (2011). *Facebook usage: Factors and analysis.* Arab Social Media Report #2. Dubai: Dubai School of Government.

Schario, T., & Konisky, D. (2008). *Public confidence in government: Trust and responsiveness.* Retrieved from http://truman.missouri.edu/ipp/publications/index.asp?.

Searson, E. M., & Johnson, M. A. (2010). Transparency laws and interactive public relations: An analysis of Latin American government Web sites. *Public Relations Review, 36*(2), 120–126. doi: 10.1016/j.pubrev.2010.03.003.

Sifry, M. (2011). *From Howard Dean to the tea party: The power of meetup.com.* Retrieved from http://www.cnn.com/2011/11/07/tech/web/meetup-2012-campaign-sifry/.

Sunstein, C. R. (2007). *Republic.Com 2.0.* Princeton, NJ: Princeton University Press.

Takaragawa, S., & Carty, V. (2012). The 2008 U.S. Presidential election and new digital technologies: Political campaigns as social movements and the significance of collective identity. *Tamara: Journal for Critical Organization Inquiry, 10*(4), 73-89.

Tiffen, R. (1989). *News & Power.* Sydney: Allen & Unwin.

Torres, L. (2007). Citizen sourcing in the public interest. *Knowledge Management for Development Journal, 3*(1), 134–145.

Wagner, K., & Gainous, J. (2009). Electronic grassroots: Does online campaigning work. *Journal of Legislative Studies, 15*(4), 502-520. doi:10.1080/13572330903302539.

Warner, B. R., & Neville-Shepard, R. M. (2011). The polarizing influence of fragmented media: Lessons from Howard Dean. *Atlantic Journal of Communication, 19,* 201-215. doi: 10.1080/15456870.2011.606100.

Waters, R. D., & Williams, J. M. (2011). Squawking, tweeting, cooing, and hooting: Analyzing the communication patterns of government agencies on Twitter. *Journal of Public Affairs, 11*(4), 353–363. doi:10.1002/pa.385.

Weinberg, B., & Williams, C. (2006). The 2004 U.S. Presidential campaign: Impact of hybrid offline and online "meetup" communities. *Journal of Direct, Data and Digital Marketing Practice, 8*(1), 46-57. doi:10.1057/palgrave.dddmp.4340552.

White, D. M. (1950). The gatekeeper: A case study in the selection of news. *Journalism Quarterly, 27,* 383–390.

Woolley, J., Limperos, A., & Oliver, M. (2010). The 2008 presidential election, 2.0: A content analysis of user-generated political Facebook groups. *Mass Communication and Society, 13,* 631-652. doi:10.1080/15205436.2010.516864.

Wolf, G. (2004). *How the Internet invented Howard Dean.* Retrieved from http://www .wired.com/wired/archive/12.01/dean_pr.html.

Zhuo, X., Wellman, B., & Yu, J. (2011). Egypt: The first Internet revolt? *Peace Magazine*. Retrieved from http://peacemagazine.org/archive/v27n3p06.htm.

FIVE

Social Media Privacy and Security

With rapid technological advancement, things that were once private knowledge have now become public. Social network sites usually encourage users to disclose a great deal of information about themselves (Antheunis, Valkenburg, & Peter, 2010), including private information such as date of birth, age, religion and political views, relationship status, and sexual preferences (Gross & Acquisti, 2005). This information could be accessed by anyone, including supervisors, strangers, and even friends who do not have good intentions. There have been multiple reported cases of employees being dismissed due to their Facebook posts, comments, photos, and the types of groups that they were linked with. One was Caitlin Davis, an 18-year-old cheerleader with the New England Patriots, who was fired over photos that she posted on Facebook. In a 2013 Pew Research Center study about anonymity, privacy, and security online, 1 percent of participants said that they have lost a job opportunity or educational opportunity because of something they posted online or someone posted about them. The survey included 1,002 adults aged 18 and older. Of those, 21 percent have had their e-mail or social network account compromised or taken over by someone else without permission (Rainie, Kiesler, Kang, & Madden, 2013).

PRIVACY PARADOX

While many citizens express concern that the government has too much information about them, they still voluntarily disclose a lot of personal data on social network sites. This is what researchers call a "privacy paradox" (Norberg, Horne, & Horne, 2007). It can be explained from a psychological perspective. People disclose because they have a need to be part of their social group. They want to be popular (Christofides, Muise,

73

& Desmarais, 2009). Therefore, Marwick and boyd (2014) emphasized that we should not study privacy as an individualistic model, but as networked privacy. Privacy cannot be entirely maintained by individuals (Marwick & boyd, 2014), as our friends can post embarrassing comments under our posts, or they can share unflattering photos of us that we would have never posted on a social network site. Most social network site users have different groups of individuals with whom they share certain information. Often it is the trust and respect that decide who gets to see the post.

PRIVACY CONCERNS

In a recent study (Stieger, Burger, Bohn, & Voracek, 2013) comparing Facebook users and Facebook quitters from all over the world, the main reason for deactivating the Facebook account were privacy concerns (48 percent). Those who quit, however, were significantly older than those who kept using Facebook, and were men (72 percent) more often than women. In a Reason-Rupe poll (2013) about how Americans felt about privacy, more Americans trusted the Internal Revenue Service than Facebook. Over 6 in 10 Americans said that they do not trust Facebook "at all" to protect their privacy, and another 15 percent said they only trust Facebook "a little." For comparison, 45 percent of Americans said that they do not trust the IRS to protect their privacy at all and 18 percent trust the IRS a little (Ekins, 2013). Despite all of the privacy settings on Facebook, most people are not aware that social network sites track their interests and likes and then, based on that information, post advertisements on their profile page. Thus, they are victims of a "social media privacy trap." Facebook, for example, will show you what products and services your friends like, in order for you to like the same pages.

Liu, Gummadi, Krishnamurthy, and Mislove (2011) measured Facebook users' disparity between the desired and actual privacy settings. They found that Facebook privacy settings matched users' expectations only 37 percent of the time. In other words, there is not enough transparency when it comes to Facebook privacy settings. Similarly, Madejski, Johnson, and Bellovin (2011) did a study to compare whether or not the users' Facebook privacy settings matched what the users intended the privacy settings to be. In the study, every single participant confirmed that at least one of the potential violations contradicted their sharing intentions. The study also suggested improving current default privacy settings.

Responding to citizens' privacy concerns related to social media use, Tyler Droll and Brooks Buffington created an anonymous social media app called Yik Yak. Yik Yak allows users to create and view "Yaks" within a radius of several miles. This way they have a chance to talk with people who are physically nearby. Yik Yak is similar to Twitter, but it has a GPS function and is completely anonymous. Some predict that anonymity is the future of social media, while others warn about cyberbullying issues that might happen as a result of that (Fye, 2014). Still, just like other social media applications, Yik Yak can share information collected about the users, including their comments—which can be reposted on Facebook, Twitter, or Instagram. Yik Yak can disclose the information in order to comply with the law, a judicial proceeding, or court orders (yikyakapp.com, 2014). It can also share aggregate or deidentified information about users with third parties for marketing or research purposes.

HUMAN RESOURCES AND PRIVACY

In a study looking at college students' opinions about employers checking their social media profiles, 68 percent of students who took the survey did not believe it was unethical for employers to look at their SNSs (Clark & Roberts, 2010). This high percentage might indicate a generational shift in what accepted use of social media is. Using social media to make employment decisions can create confusion because of a lack of clarity about whether content posted to social media sites is public or private (Aase, 2010). Employers can use information found on social media sites as part of their hiring process because publicly searchable information is not considered private (Brown & Vaughn, 2011). However, to what extent employees can be dismissed based on inappropriate use of social media depends on national legislation. In the last couple of years, some employers have asked employees or prospective hires to disclose their social media usernames and passwords. In some states lawmakers have introduced legislation that would prevent employers from such practices. As of December 2014, legislation has been introduced or is pending in 28 states. It was enacted in seven others in 2014 and ten states in 2013. In Louisiana, the Governor signed the Personal Online Account Privacy Protection Act, which prohibits employers and educational institutions from requesting individuals to disclose information that allows access to their personal online accounts (NCSL, 2014).

Law enforcement increasingly uses social media to solve crimes. In some cases, police violate Facebook policy by creating fake profiles that help them learn more about the suspects (Kelly, 2012). Civil liberties groups such as the Electronic Frontier Foundation are against such practices that challenge the idea that users have no right to privacy for information stored online (Kelly, 2012). According to a survey of 1,200 federal, state, and local law enforcement professionals, one out of five respondents used various social media platforms to assist in investigations. More than half believed that social media helps them solve crimes more quickly (LexisNexis, 2012). In some cases, criminals use social media carelessly, often to plot the crimes and even to brag about wrongdoings (Kelly, 2012).

YOUNG ADULTS' VIEWS REGARDING ONLINE PRIVACY AND SECURITY

In a 2013 Pew Research Study (Madden, Lenhart, Cortesi, Gasser, Duggan, Smith, & Beaton) of teen privacy on social media, 60 percent of teen Facebook users stated that they keep their profiles private. Only 16 percent of teens have set up their profile to automatically include their location in posts, according to the study. In addition, 74 percent of teens have deleted people from their network or friend list as one of the privacy management techniques. While these numbers seem encouraging, the study found that teens do not practice the same behavior on Twitter. Unlike Facebook, Twitter does not have all the privacy settings, and the user can either protect their tweets, or keep them public. Unlike on Facebook, there are no other options. Another concern of the study results is the fact that most teen social media users (60 percent) wrongfully believed that Facebook does not share their information with third parties.

Overall, adolescents tend to "overshare" online simply because they are unaware of the consequences (Walrave, Vanwesenbeeck, & Heirman, 2012). That is why they have lower levels of privacy settings on SNSs. What many adults consider private information, adolescents readily disclose on social media. However, those users who have little trust in their friend list contacts feel less inclined to disclose personal information and more inclined to apply stricter privacy settings (Patil, 2012). Lower levels of trust in other SNS members is a significant indicator of higher levels of information control (Christofides et al., 2009). Contrary to expectations and popular media articles, Christofides et al. (2009) found that information disclosure and information control were not significantly negatively correlated. Disclosure was the result of a need for popularity and a general tendency to disclose, while self-esteem and levels of trust predicted information control. Students in their study were generally concerned about their privacy, and researchers concluded that they disclose the types of information that other users disclose. This relates to theory of reasoned action (Ajzen & Fishbein, 1980), which suggests that a person's behavior is determined by his or her intention to perform the behavior, and that this intention is, in turn, a function of his or her attitude toward the behavior and his or her subjective norm. Subjective norm is the "perceived social pressure to perform or not to perform the behavior" (Ajzen, 1991). This social pressure might come from peers, family, school, or the workplace and can be the reason students feel pressure to be open about their lives.

In chapter 3, we explored the quest for fame, which is a related reason for why adolescents disclose on Facebook. In "nonymous" environments such as Facebook, individuals prefer to show rather than tell others about themselves (Zhao, Grasmuck, & Martin, 2008). In fact, when it comes to young adults, most are concerned about controlling what their parents can see (boyd, 2007). Often, they create separate audience groups who can see their posts, while they limit them for others. Teens can also write in crypts that only their closest friends can understand. boyd and Marwick (2011) introduced the term "social steganography," which means hiding messages. The idea of steganography is to communicate only to a particular segment of friends. For example, in Peluchette and Karl's study (2008), 20 percent of participants said that they would not be comfortable if employers see certain information on their Facebook page. The most commonly listed items that students did not want their employers to see were alcohol-related photos or comments. Some students did not want them to see inappropriate humor jokes or comments left by friends. Again, men indicated less concern than women. In terms of sex, research shows that women are more protective of their social media privacy and have greater restrictions on their profiles (Walrave, Vanwesenbeeck, & Heirman, 2012). Peluchette and Karl (2008) also found that men were more likely than women to post self-promoting and risqué pictures or comments (involving sex or alcohol) on their profile. Females were more likely than males to post romantic or "cute" pictures.

Other studies have also found a positive association between privacy-related concerns and the application of stricter privacy settings (Utz & Kramer, 2009; Nov & Wattal, 2009). Although today's teens disclose personal information that their parents often regarded as private (e.g., age, politics, religion, sexual preferences), they are still aware of the risks of putting information online (Utz & Kramer, 2009). Livingstone (2008) argued that their definition of privacy has changed; thus, it is not being tied to disclosing certain types of information, but for them privacy is about control and who knows what about them. This is related to teens restricting their SNS profiles so that parents cannot see some of the content.

Another negative aspect of social media use includes high school and college students making drug and alcohol references for the public—and future employers—to see. Egan and Moreno (2011) conducted a study examining alcohol references on undergrad males' Facebook profiles. The study found that students who were of legal drinking age referenced alcohol 4.5 times more than underage students. Out of all the profiles, 85.3 percent contained alcohol references. Egan and Moreno (2011) argued that such depiction of alcohol-related events could be damaging to personal and professional reputations.

COMMUNICATION PRIVACY MANAGEMENT THEORY

Recently, communication privacy management theory (Petronio, 2002) has been used to explain the "privacy paradox," or why users disclose personal information on social network sites while at the same time expressing concerns about privacy (see chapter 1 for a more detailed discussion). Petronio (2002, p. 6) defines privacy "as the feeling that one has the right to own private information, either personally or collectively." When a person shares private information, others become its co-owners. That can potentially lead to privacy turbulence, or intentionally violating the established rules by disclosing private information that was supposed to be confidential. Another privacy management technique for controlling who sees what and when is the practice of friending, unfriending, and blocking SNS friends (Madden et al., 2013). According to a study, 74 percent of teen social media users have deleted people from their network of friends list. This shows that they think proactively in terms of who they want to share the information with.

Professors and educators deal with privacy dialectics on a daily basis when trying to decide which information to reveal to their students on social network profiles—and which to conceal. Despite anecdotal evidence of teachers adding students as friends on online social networks, there has been almost no research studying privacy concerns that teachers might have. Some researchers (Cain & Fink, 2010) have argued that the overexposure to each other's private lives might have negative consequences for the faculty member, as students often do not appreciate their presence on SNSs (Hewitt & Forte, 2006). Media outlets have reported cases of elementary, high school, and college instructors being fired for something that they posted publicly on their social network profile. According to the American Association of University Professors' (AAUP) ethical principles and standards, college personnel should "avoid dual relationships with students where one individual serves in multiple roles that create conflicting responsibilities, role confusion, and unclear expectations that may involve incompatible roles and conflicting responsibilities" (ACPA Ethics Code, 2006).

REFERENCES

Aase, S. (2010). Toward e-professionalism: thinking through the implications of navigating the digital world. *Journal of the American Dietetic Association, 110*(10), 1442-1447. doi:10.1016/j.jada.2010.08.020.

ACPA Ethics Code (2006). *Statement of ethical principles and standards*. Retrieved from http://www.myacpa.org/au/documents/EthicsStatement.pdf.

Ajzen, I. (1991). The theory of planned behavior. *Organization Behavior and Human Decision Processes, 50*, 179-211. doi:10.1016/0749-5978(91)90020-T.

Ajzen, I., & Fishbein, M. (1980). *Understanding attitudes and predicting social behavior.* Englewood Cliffs, NJ: Prentice-Hall.

Antheunis, M. L., Valkenburg, P. M., & Peter, J. (2010). Getting acquainted through social network sites: Testing a model of online uncertainty reduction and social attraction. *Computers in Human Behavior, 26*, 100-109. doi:10.1016/j.chb.2009.07.005.

boyd, d. m. (2007). Why youth (heart) social network sites: The role of networked publics in teenage social life. In Buckingham, D. (Ed.), *McArthur Foundation series on digital learning—Youth, identity, and digital media volume.* Cambridge, MA: MIT Press.

boyd, d. m., & Marwick, A. (2011) Social privacy in networked publics: teens' attitudes, practices, and strategies. Paper presented at the Oxford Internet Institute Decade in Internet Time Symposium.

Brown, V. R., & Vaughn, E. D. (2011).The writing on the (Facebook) wall: The use of social networking sites in hiring decisions. *Journal of Business Psychology, 26*, 219-225. doi:10.1007/s10869-011-9221-x.

Cain, J., & Fink, J. L. (2010). Legal and ethical issues regarding social media and pharmacy education. *American Journal of Pharmaceutical Education, 74*(10), 1-7. doi:10.5688/aj7410184.

Christofides, E., Muise, A., & Desmarais, S. (2009). Information disclosure and control on Facebook: Are they two sides of the same coin or two different processes? *CyberPsychology & Behavior, 12*, 341-345. doi:10.1089/cpb.2008.0226.

Clark, L., & Roberts, S. (2010). Employer's use of social networking sites: A socially irresponsible practice. *Journal of Business Ethics, 95*(4), 507-525. doi:10.1007/s10551-010-0436-y.

Egan, K., & Moreno, M. (2011). Alcohol references on undergraduate males' Facebook profiles. *American Journal of Men's Health, 5*, 413-420. doi:10.1177/1557988310394341.

Ekins, E. (2013). *Poll: On privacy, IRS, and NSA deemed more trustworthy than Facebook and Google.* Retrieved from http://reason.com/poll/2013/09/27/poll-on-privacy-irs-and-nsa-deemed-more.

Fye, S. (2014). Yik Yak: Why it exists. *The Atlas Business Journal.* Retrieved from http://atlasbusinessjournal.org/yik-yak-greater-implications-upon-society/.

Gross, R., & Acquisti, A. (2005). Information revelation and privacy in online social networks. Proceedings of the 2005 ACM workshop on privacy in the electronic society, 71-80.

Hewitt, A., & Forte, A. (2006). *Crossing boundaries: Identity management and student/faculty relationships on Facebook.* Poster presented at the Computer Supported Cooperative Work (CSCW).

Kelly, H. (2012, August 30). *Police embrace social media as crime-fighting tool.* Retrieved from http://www.cnn.com/2012/08/30/tech/social-media/fighting-crime-social-media/.

LexisNexis (2012). *Role of social media in law enforcement significant and growing.* Retrieved from http://www.lexisnexis.com/en-us/about-us/media/press-release.page?id=1342623085481181.

Liu, Y., Gummadi, K., Krishnamurthy, B., & Mislove, A. (2011). Analyzing Facebook privacy settings: User expectations vs. reality. In *Proceedings of the 2011 ACM SIGCOMM conference on Internet measurement conference*, 61-70.

Livingstone, S. (2008). Taking risky opportunities in youthful content creation: Teenagers' use of social networking sites for intimacy, privacy, and self-expression. *New Media & Society, 10*, 339-411. doi:10.1177/1461444808089415.

Madden, M., Lenhart, A., Cortesi, S., Gasser, U., Duggan, M., Smith, A., & Beaton, M. (2013, May 21). *Teens, social media, and privacy.* Retrieved November 1, 2014, from http://www.pewinternet.org/2013/05/21/teens-social-media-and-privacy/#.

Madejski, M., Johnson, M., & Bellovin, S. (2011).The failure of online social network privacy settings. *Columbia University Computer Science Technical Reports.* Retrieved from http://academiccommons.columbia.edu/catalog/ac:135406.

Marwick, A. E., & boyd, d. (2014). Networked privacy: How teenagers negotiate context in social media. *New Media & Society, 16*(7), 1051-1067. doi:10.1177/1461444814543995.

NCSL (2014). Employer access to social media usernames and passwords. Retrieved from http://www.ncsl.org/research/telecommunications-and-information-technolo-gy/employer-access-to-social-media-passwords-2013.aspx.

Norberg, P. A., Horne, D. R., & Horne, D. A. (2007). The privacy paradox: Personal information disclosure intentions versus behaviors. *Journal of Consumer Affairs, 41,* 100–126. doi:10.1111/j.1745-6606.2006.00070.x.

Nov, O., & Wattal, S. (2009). *Social computing privacy concerns: antecedents and effects.* Paper presented at 27th International Conference on Human Factors in Computing Systems.

Patil, S. (2012). *Will you be my friend?: Responses to friendship requests from strangers.* Proceedings of the 2012 iConference.

Peluchette, J., & Karl, K. (2008). Social networking profiles: An examination of student attitudes regarding use and appropriateness of content. *CyberPsychology & Behavior, 11,* 95–7. doi:10.1089/cpb.2007.9927.

Petronio, S. (2002). *Boundaries of privacy: Dialectics of disclosure.* New York: State University of New York Press.

Rainie, L., Kiesler, S., Kang, R., & Madden, M. (2013). Anonymity, privacy, and security online. *Pew Research Internet Project.* Retrieved from http://www.pewinternet.org/2013/09/05/anonymity-privacy-and-security-online/.

Stieger, S., Burger, C., Bohn, M., & Voracek, M. (2013). Who commits virtual identity suicide? Differences in privacy concerns, Internet addiction, and personality between Facebook users and quitters. *Cyberpsychology, Behavior, and Social Networking, 16,* 629-634. doi:10.1089/cyber.2012.0323.

Utz, S., & Kramer, N. (2009). The privacy paradox on social network sites revisited: The role of individual characteristics and group norms. *Cyberpsychology: Journal of Psychosocial Research on Cyberspace, 3*(2), article 1.

Walrave, M., Vanwesenbeeck, I., & Heirman, W. (2012). Connecting and protecting? Comparing predictors of self-disclosure and privacy settings use between adolescents and adults. *Cyberpsychology: Journal of Psychosocial Research on Cyberspace, 6*(1), article 3.

YikYak (2014). *Privacy.* Retrieved from http://www.yikyakapp.com/privacy/.

Zhao, S., Grasmuck, S., & Martin, J. (2008). Identity construction on Facebook: Digital empowerment in anchored relationships. *Computers in Human Behavior, 24,* 1816-36. doi:10.1016/j.chb.2008.02.012.

SIX

Social Media in Education

The traditional classroom environment includes an instructor and a student. The role of the instructor is to communicate the course content. This process is mostly one-way. New communication technologies have created opportunities for learning to be interactive and less focused on the instructor. For example, social media allow both instructors and students to communicate between and among each other in and out of class. However, a number of studies have warned about teachers not being prepared for the use of social media in the classroom. Many teachers remain concerned about cyber safety and exam cheating (Sharples, Graber, Harrison, & Logant, 2008), privacy, but also longer working hours (Lepi, 2013). While most students are eager to use social media during class, instructors are slow in adopting it (Queirolo, 2009). In order for social media to be incorporated into instruction, instructors not only have to change how they teach, but they also need to be trained to use social media as instructional technologies (Keengwe, Kidd, & Kyei-Blankson, 2009; Long, 2009).

This chapter explores both the benefits and challenges of using social media in education. It reports the results of experimental studies supporting the use of blogs, YouTube, and Twitter in the college classroom. It further explains the dynamics of student-teacher relationship on Facebook, and it finishes with a discussion of e-learning and the use of social media in K–12 education.

CHALLENGES AND BENEFITS OF USING SOCIAL MEDIA IN EDUCATION

Social media interrupt formal education in multiple ways, by challenging the existing preconceptions of schools, teachers, students, and learning (Bartow, 2014; Condie & Livingston, 2007). Bartow (2014) argued that social technologies present educational, ethical, economic, and revolutionary changes in the organization and structure of schools. One of the educational changes includes self-directed learning. Users can choose how, when, where, and by whom they want to be educated (Bartow, 2014). This also includes the promise of an open and free exchange of ideas (Bartow, 2014). From an ethical standpoint, digital technologies incorporated in public education can help reduce the digital divide. Economically, online learning is cost-effective with the content reaching a large number of students. Finally, from a revolutionary standpoint, social media have democratized access to knowledge (Bartow, 2014).

The following are the *benefits* of using social media in education:

- More student-centered courses (Greenhow, 2011).
- Interaction with each other and instructors (Hoffman, 2009).
- Personal choice and customization (Hoffman, 2009).
- User-generated content, which allows collaborative activities including use of wikis and blogs (Gikas & Grant, 2013; Lemoine & Richardson, 2013).
- Improved access and availability; more adult students participate in the learning process (Bjerede, Atkins, & Dede, 2010).
- Increased level of engagement and interactivity among students (Nicolini, Mengis, & Swan, 2012).
- Shy students are more participatory in a less direct environment (Van Merriënboer & Stoyanov, 2008).
- Students use YouTube to share a video project or Twitter to track a particular concept (Junco, Heiberger, & Loken, 2011; Shih & Waugh, 2011).
- Opportunities for creative work and peer alumni support (Greenhow & Robelia, 2009).

USING SOCIAL MEDIA FOR RECRUITMENT AND RETENTION

Most universities and schools today use social media to recruit new students and also to share news with those already enrolled. High school students use social media to learn about prospective colleges and universities. According to a 2013 Social Admissions Report, 75 percent of students who graduated from high school in 2013 used social media as a resource when deciding where to enroll. Facebook ranked first among all social media that students checked for college information. This was followed by YouTube, Twitter, and Instagram. While 75 percent of students used social media as a resource, only 49 percent actually liked or followed the college on social media. Interestingly, the top three people students wanted to interact with were: (1) currently enrolled students; (2) admission counselors, and (3) other newly admitted students. Suggestions for improving the college presence on social media included posting more photographs, more information about scholarships and internships, more information about the incoming student process, and more videos on specific subjects and classes (*Social Admissions Report*, 2013). As evident from a survey conducted by companies that focus on school-matching services (Zinch) and a company that concentrates on student engagement online (Inigral), high school students expect a more interactive engagement with colleges social media sites. The generation of students entering colleges today grew up with digital and interactive media and, therefore, rely less on textual data. In fact, most high school students now cite Instagram as their most engaged social network site, while Facebook still has the most daily users (Thompson, 2014). This is not surprising considering that Instagram is a photo- and video-sharing site.

Social media can help not only with enrollment but retention as well. McClure (2013) cited the example of students who complain about classes on social media. Community managers and other school personnel could reach out to those students and help them before the problems exacerbate. Traditionally, students would complain to their peers face-to-face or in phone calls home, but today social media is where they broadcast their concerns (McClure, 2013). It is therefore necessary that universities create social media sites where students can communicate with other students who are taking similar classes or have similar experiences.

Education researchers have argued that fellow students are the single most important source of influences in college students' lives, and a key predictor of education outcomes—including perseverance and commitment (Astin, 1993; Broome, Croke, Staton, & Zachritz, 2012). Social media allow students to share and exchange ideas online. It is especially critical during the first year of college when students are trying to make new friends, to adjust to campus and college life (Galindo, Bogran Meling, Mundy, & Kupczynski, 2012). Hernandez, Newman, and Lopez (2014) suggested that colleges should use Facebook effectively—which includes liking pages that relate to their goals and audience, posting at appropriate times for their audiences' schedules, and tagging other pages to target and increase the impact. Colleges should also promote their Facebook pages through offline avenues, use different types of posts to keep pages dynamic, connect Facebook to other venues, and be creative. Hernandez et al.'s (2014) suggestion included asking incoming freshmen enrolled at a community college or public university to "like" the school's Facebook page and report the page on their Facebook wall for the opportunity to win a gift voucher. Hernandez at al. (2014) proposed that on their social media sites universities should provide tips that will make students successful in college. Live chats should also be available for students to communicate in real time with faculty, counselors, and administrators. Schools should keep score or metrics of social media use by utilizing

Facebook Analytics, Google Analytics, and YouTube Analytics, and keep track of fans and followers.

Campus leaders also encourage students to use social media to broadcast their achievements in college. According to McClure (2013), this helps publicity of the school. Ramig (2014) emphasized the importance of schools not blocking collaboration sites such as blogs, wikis, and social networks. Instead, teachers should be taught how to use them. Students need to learn to critically evaluate information that they find on the Internet, as well as how to be safe online and how to appropriately use different sites.

SOCIAL MEDIA IN THE CLASSROOM

The Babson Survey Research Group and Pearson conducted a survey of 8,000 faculty members in higher education to learn how faculty are using social media. Lepi (2013) reported the results that show the level of personal use of social media among faculty (70 percent) mirrors that of the general population. Only 41 percent of the faculty used social media in the classroom. Chen and Bryer (2012) explored the use of social media among faculty in the discipline of public administration in the United States. Instructors in their study perceived that the informal learning using social media could be integrated into a formal learning environment. Faculty believed that students could exercise their creativity by using images, videos, and audios. LinkedIn was seen as a great tool to network with alumna and future employers. Some instructors had already used YouTube videos and case studies from wiki pages, and others incorporated blogging as part of the class discussions. However, the major concerns still remained: cybersecurity and privacy issues. Some faculty felt reluctant to friend their students, fearing inappropriate personal disclosures, and others worried about students posting inappropriate content. For many senior faculty, time constraints and technology barriers were the biggest concern. Chen and Bryer (2012) conclude that faculty should experiment with social media, and institutions should facilitate such experimentation.

Although social media platforms are not specifically designed for classroom use, professors are using them to communicate with their students out of class as well as to create learning opportunities. Students are also sharing course material with each other through social network sites. In the early days of social media (2000–2010), professors and students were using blogs or online journals to comment on and discuss the course material (Anderson, 2007). However, microblogging replaced regular blogging by 2011. Currently, Twitter is the most popular microblogging site that professors and students use to hashtag and retweet related links and ask questions about course material (McEwan, 2012). Although not all instructors use Twitter in their classes, research shows that microblogging increases student engagement and improves academic outcomes (Junco, 2011; Schirmer, 2011). Many students use social media to reach out for mentoring or to stay in touch with professors once the course has ended (Helvie-Mason, 2011; Sheldon, 2014). LinkedIn is the perfect place for such professional connections. Another possibility is a Facebook group where students can join and talk to their instructor (Helvie-Mason, 2011). According to Liu, Kalk, Kinney, and Orr (2009), the most commonly used social media technologies in higher education are blogs, podcasts, social networking, and virtual environments. We will first discuss the use of blogs as an educational tool.

Blogs

Several researchers (e.g., Churchill, 2009; Harrison, 2011; Sim & Hew, 2010; Deng & Yuen, 2011) have examined blogs as an educational tool in higher education classes. Based on a review of 24 articles, Sim and Hew (2010) found six major uses of blogs: (1) a learning journal for gathering or reporting course-related information; (2) a record of personal life; (3) an outlet for expressing emotions and feelings; (4) a communication tool for social interaction with other people; (5) an assessment tool for peer evaluation; and 6) a task management tool for posting assignments.

Sim and Hew (2010) also reviewed studies focusing on the effects of blogging on participants' learning and thinking skills. While most studies were self-reports, the authors found that the use of blogs could help student learning. For some students, blogs provided a space to reflect and comment (Xie, Ke, & Sharma, 2008). For students who remain silent during class discussions, blogs are the place to contribute their thoughts. Blogs can also be used as digital portfolios for student assignments (Liu & Chang, 2010). Yang and Chang (2011) conducted an experiment with both undergraduate and graduate students to explore the use of blogs and how student attitudes toward online peer interaction and peer learning—as well as motivation to learn from peers—differ when students are using the blog comments feature versus reading and commenting on each other's work. Their results showed that the interactive use of blogs in higher education, when compared with the option of using a blog in isolation, was related to more positive attitudes toward online peer interaction among learners, as well as higher academic achievements.

College students also benefit from blogging about class topics (Churchill, 2009; Harrison, 2011). Blogging increases students' engagement in course material and makes students feel that their opinions matter. Blogs were seen as effective when students had a chance to reflect on the posted content, as well as to comment on their peer contributions (Churchill, 2009). Even older technologies such as e-mail, lecture notes in pdf, and online discussion forums can be used with the new Web 2.0

technologies—such as student blogs, a class wiki project, a Twitter discussion, or a video presentation on YouTube (Friedman & Friedman, 2013). According to Friedman and Friedman (2013), the best of all delivery methods is still a hybrid course that combines traditional classroom learning with online learning.

Twitter

Twitter can be a smart instructional tool if used correctly. Journell, Ayers, and Beeson (2014) reported the findings of a study looking at how a high school civics course used Twitter during the 2012 presidential election. They found that Twitter allowed students to participate in an academic discussion through a format that they prefer and like. Carton (2014) discussed the advantages of Twitter for educators' professional development. Unlike Facebook, most people do not use Twitter to post pictures of their kids, or to describe what they had for dinner. Instead, they are following education-related posts. Another great feature of Twitter is that people can easily unfollow others as their interests evolve. Retweeting can also be helpful as other people might find the links helpful. In a Journell et al. (2014) study, students created Twitter accounts at the beginning of the semester. The teacher required students to follow both major party presidential candidates. The teacher created a unique hashtag (#chscivics) for students to use while they tweeted during each event. Hashtags helped other students see their tweets. Hashtags also allowed students to connect with classrooms across the United States. Journell et al. (2014) argued that this is an example of an authentic instruction that helps connect one's curriculum to the world beyond the classroom (Newmann & Wehlage, 1993).

Junco et al. (2011) found that using Twitter in educationally relevant ways had a positive effect on student engagement as well as their grades. The results showed that students were motivated and engaged with each other, but were also enthusiastic about collaborative learning on their service project through study groups organized via Twitter. Twitter also helped not-so-active participants in class to participate online. In my own social media class, students tweet discussion questions related to the reading for that class period. My observation has been that students monitor each other's questions and often come up with follow-up questions based on the question posted by another student. This practice helps students think critically and creatively as students are asked to think of questions of application to a practical situation and questions of challenge where real-life experience contradicts what research has shown.

Since Twitter was not created for educational purposes solely, there are limitations of using this social medium, including inappropriate commenting and bullying (Journell et al., 2014). Journell et al. (2014) suggest that teachers need to establish rules for tweeting the same way they establish rules for a traditional classroom discussion. Also, in their study, students did not seem to respond to each other's tweets and were talking "at each other, rather than with each other" (p. 66).

Facebook

While Twitter and blogs are often used solely for learning purposes, Facebook is seen as a network where students and faculty could establish a more informal out-of-class relationship. For many faculty, however, this relationship remains controversial as in some cases students do not think that faculty should be present on social media to "spy" on their lives, and, in other cases, faculty do not feel that students should have access to their private lives (Cain, Scott, & Akers, 2009; Hewitt & Forte, 2006). Many faculty express ethical concerns (ACPA Ethics Code, 2006) when adding students as friends, especially worrying about role confusion, conflicting responsibilities, and incompatible roles that might contribute to unacceptable dual relationships. Some scholars (McEwan, 2012) have argued that faculty should never initiate relationships with students on social networks and should wait until students add them, while others (e.g., Jones, 2011) have emphasized that faculty should not use them for hanging out with students online, but rather for learning purposes. However, some (e.g., Schwartz, 2009) have mentioned that Facebook friendships with students meet the criteria of a mentoring relationship that helps students feel connected to an instructor.

Social network sites, if used correctly, do promote learning inside and outside the classroom. The U.S. Supreme Court has also supported the contention that teachers should be protected by academic freedom in their use of social network sites to communicate with their students. This is reasonable considering studies supporting this kind of relationship. In different studies students who were friends with faculty on Facebook were more willing to interact with them offline (Sturgeon & Walker, 2009), anticipated a more positive classroom climate if a teacher self-disclosed on Facebook (Mazer, Murphy, & Simonds, 2007), had greater academic achievements (Pascarella, 1985), and a greater sense of well-being (Roorda, Koomen, Spilt, & Oort, 2011). Puzio (2013) concluded that students might reach teachers on Facebook to discuss other school-related issues such as bullying or depression, as it might be easier for a student to discuss those issues online rather than face to face. "Social network sites have the potential to serve as a powerful tool to enhance education, communication, and learning" (Puzio, 2013, p. 1120). Sheldon (2014) conducted a study to learn what motivates faculty and students to be each other's friends on Facebook. Most students would add faculty in order to get to know them better on a personal level, which reinforces DiVerniero and Hosek (2011) who also found that having access to the instructors' online profiles allows students to see them as "human beings" and "friends." Faculty, however, had slightly negative beliefs about what important others would think of them being a Facebook friend with a student. Many faculty members mentioned that they would add a student as a friend after he or she graduates but only if the student initiated the relationship.

Research conducted in countries outside of the United States (Draskovic, Caic, & Kustrak, 2013; Baran, 2010) also found that more students than faculty believed that it was quite appropriate for instructors and students to socialize through Facebook. Benefits included getting a fast response from lecturers and graduate assistants, as well as discussing course content and answering questions that students might have (Draskovic et al., 2013).

SOCIAL MEDIA AND ONLINE LEARNING

The efforts by faculty and students in creating new ways of teaching and learning led to the emergence of constructs such as e-learning 2.0 (Downes, 2005) and pedagogy 2.0, characterizing themes such as openness, collaboration, social networking, social presence, user-generated content (Dabbagh & Kitsantas, 2012). As a result of implementing social media in education and e-learning, the concept of PLE (personal learning environment) emerged. PLE is defined as the "tools, communities, and services that constitute the individual educational platforms that learners use to direct their own learning and pursue educational goals" (EDU-CAUSE Learning Initiative [ELI], 2009, p. 1). While traditional learning management systems (LMS) have always been under the control of the university, PLE is less structured and allows informal learning and connections to peers (Dabbagh & Kitsantas, 2012). PLE includes social media such as Facebook and YouTube, blogs, and wikis. Martindale and Dowdy (2010) argued that social media allow similar opportunities as face-to-face lunchtime discussions and study sessions.

The National Science Foundation Task Force on Cyberlearning defines cyberlearning as learning that is mediated by networked computing and communications technologies (2008). This includes social media and other emerging forms of technology (Lemoine & Richardson, 2013) that can help students learn by doing (Jones, Morales, & Knezek, 2005). Instead of being the sole source of knowledge, an instructor could now be a facilitator that can help support student learning (Mishra, Lemoine, Campbell, Mense, & Richardson, 2013).

The number of students taking online courses continues to grow, with 30 percent of college students taking at least one class online (Allen & Seaman, 2010; as cited in Friedman & Friedman, 2013). Many colleges prefer online courses as it saves them money. Friedman and Friedman (2013) suggested that social media could be used to make homework fun and useful. Online learning, according to them, offers many advantages over traditional classroom learning, resulting in a better performance for students. Online learning, however, requires students to be active participants in the learning environment, creating it and communicating with one another.

Some argue (e.g., Carey, 2012) that MOOCs (Massive Open Online Courses) will soon change the future of higher education. The idea of the MOOC is unlimited, open access via the web. In 2011, Stanford offered three MOOC courses. Enrollment in "Introduction to Artificial Intelligence," offered by Sebastian Thrun, quickly reached several hundred students. Many MOOC classes use video lectures, or what is considered the old form of teaching. One type of lecture design includes the flipped classroom approach. In a flipped classroom, students watch lectures online at home and work on projects while in class.

SOCIAL MEDIA AND COLLECTIVE INTELLIGENCE

Some scholars (e.g., O'Reilly & Battelle, 2009) have argued that social media technologies, such as blogs, wikis, and social network sites, can facilitate content that is co-created by and for the community and represents "collective intelligence." Thompson, Gray, and Kim (2014) empirically tested the assumption that social media promote collective intelligence. Their focus groups with 20 students revealed no evidence of "collective intelligence." Students who completed assignments using various forms of social media technologies still described their learning using a first person singular pronoun ("I").

Another study explored the relationship between Facebook use and student engagement, using a large sample (N = 2,368) of college students (Junco, 2012). Engagement was defined as "the amount of physical and psychological energy that the student devotes to the academic experience" (Astin, 1984, p. 297). The results showed that time spent on Facebook was negatively predictive of student engagement. However, some communicative activities (commenting and creating or RSVPing to events) were positively related to engagement, while non-communicative activities (playing games) were negatively related. Communicative activities on Facebook were also positively related to time spent in co-curriculum activities, while non-communicative activities were negatively predictive of time spent in co-curriculum activities. Junco (2012) concluded that students use Facebook in various ways and that can positively or negatively predict their academic outcomes.

USING SOCIAL MEDIA IN K-12 EDUCATION

Using social media in K-12 education might be different from using social media in higher education. Huffman (2013) suggests that both teachers and students should be trained to plan the use of technology in the classroom. She suggests that teachers should never use their personal accounts with students or parents, citing Greenhow (2009) who advised that day-to-day trials and tribulations should not be shared in a virtual setting in the same way they are not shared in a traditional classroom setting.

Mao (2014) conducted a mixed-methods design study to learn how high school students use social media, their attitudes and beliefs about these technologies, as well as how social media can be used in education. Mao (2014) found that most high school students use social media for entertaining, getting connected with friends and family, and sharing pictures and videos. The least mentioned reasons were things related to school work or learning. Students, however, said that using social media in education could be fun, but it is not often done. Most of their teachers use YouTube videos, but that is all. This frustrates students who believe that social media are used inappropriately in classes. Some mentioned that YouTube videos were pointless and were used to teach in lieu of the teacher. They recommend that instructors use social media in a more interactive and thoughtful way (e.g., a person who survived the Holocaust could be interviewed through Skype). Students, themselves use social media to get instant help with their homework from peers, to do research for class projects, as well as to use supplemental resources for textbooks (Mao, 2014).

REFERENCES

ACPA Ethics Code (2006). *Statement of ethical principles and standards.* Retrieved from http://www.myacpa.org/au/documents/EthicsStatement.pdf.

Allen, I. E., & Seaman, J. (2010, November). Class differences: Online education in the United States, 2010. *Sloan Consortium.* Retrieved from http://sloanconsortium.org /publications/survey/class_differences.

Anderson, P. (2007). What is Web 2.0? Ideas, technologies, and implications for education. *JISC Report.* Retrieved from www.jisc.ac.uk./media/documents/techwatch /tsw0701b.pdf.

Astin, A. (1993). *What matters in college? Four critical years revisited.* Jossey-Bass.

Astin, A. (1984). Student involvement: A developmental theory for higher education. *Journal of College Student Personnel, 25*(4), 297-308.

Baran, B. (2010). Facebook as a formal instructional environment. *British Journal of Educational Technology, 41,* 146-149. doi:10.1111/j.1467-8535.2010.01115.x.

Bartow, S. M. (2014). Teaching with social media: Disrupting present day public education. *Educational Studies: A Journal of the American Educational Studies Association, 50,* 36-64. doi:10.1080/00131946.2013.866954.

Bjerede, M., Atkins, K., & Dede, C. (2010). Ubiquitous mobile technologies and the transformation of schooling. *Educational Technology, 50*(2), 3-7.

Broome, R., Croke, B., Staton, M., & Zachritz, H. (2012). The social side of student retention. *Inigral Insights*. Retrieved from http://www.10000degrees.org/wp-content/uploads/2012/11/The_Social_Side_of_Student_Retention.pdf.

Cain, J., Scott, D. R., & Akers, P. (2009). Pharmacy students' Facebook activity and opinions regarding accountability and e-professionalism. *American Journal of Pharmaceutical Education, 73*(6), 1-6.

Carey, K. (2012, September 7). Into the future with MOOC's. *Chronicle of Higher Education, 59*, A136.

Carton, M. T. (2014). Twitter PD. *Illinois Reading Council Journal, 42*, 25-27.

Chen, B., & Bryer, T. (2012). Investigating instructional strategies for using social media in formal and informal learning. *The International Review of Research in Open and Distance Learning, 13*, 87-104.

Churchill, D. (2009). Educational applications of Web 2.0: Using blogs to support teaching and learning. *British Journal of Educational Technology, 40*, 179–183.

Condie, R., & Livingston, K. (2007). Blending online learning with traditional approaches: Changing practices. *British Journal of Educational Technology, 38*, 337–348.

Dabbagh, N., & Kitsantas, A. (2012). Personal learning environments, social media, and self-regulated learning: A natural formula for connecting formal and informal learning. *Internet and Higher Education, 15*, 3-8. doi:10.1016/j.iheduc.2011.06.002.

Deng, L., & Yuen, A. H. K. (2011). Towards a framework for educational affordances of blogs. *Computers & Education, 56*(2), 441-451. doi:10.1016/j.compedu.2010.09.005.

DiVerniero, R.A., & Hosek, A. M. (2011). Students' perceptions and communicative management of instructors' online self-disclosure. *Communication Quarterly, 59*, 428-449. doi:10.1080/01463373.2011.597275.

Downes S. (2005). E-learning 2.0. *eLearn magazine: Education and technology in perspective*. Retrieved from http://www.elearnmag.org/subpage.cfm?section=articles&article=29-1.

Draskovic, N., Caic, M., & Kustrak, A. (2013). Croatian perspective(s) on the lecturer-student interaction through social media. *International Journal of Management Cases, 15*(4), 331-339.

EDUCAUSE Learning Initiative (2009). *Seven things you should know about personal learning environments*. Retrieved from http://www.educause.edu/library/resources/7-things-you-should-know-about-personal-learning-environments.

Friedman, L., & Friedman, H. H. (2013). Using social media technologies to enhance online learning. *Journal of Educators Online, 10*(1). Retrieved from http://files.eric.ed.gov/fulltext/EJ1004891.pdf.

Galindo, A. M., Bogran Meling, V., Mundy, M., & Kupczynski, L. (2012). Social media and retention: The administrative perspective at Hispanic-serving institutions of higher education. *Journal of Studies in Education, 2*, 103-115. doi:10.5296/jse.v2i3.1809.

Gikas, J., & Grant, M. M. (2013). Mobile computing devices in higher education: Student perspectives on learning with cellphones, smartphones & social media. *Internet & Higher Education, 19*, 18-26. doi:10.1016/j.iheduc.2013.06.002.

Greenhow, C. (2009). Social scholarship: Apply social networking technologies to research practices. *Knowledge Quest, 37*(4), 42-48.

Greenhow, C. (2011.) Online social networks and learning." *On the Horizon, 19*(1), 4-12.

Greenhow, C., & Robelia, B. (2009). Old communication, new literacies: Social network sites as social learning resources. *Journal of Computer-Mediated Communication, 14*, 1130–1161. doi:10.1111/j.1083-6101.2009.01484.x.

Harrison, D. (2011). *Can blogging make a difference?: Campus Technology*. Retrieved from http://campustechnology.com/articles/2011/01/12/can-blogging-make-a-difference.aspx.

Helvie-Mason, L. (2011). Facebook, 'friending,' and faculty–student communication. In C. Wankel (Ed.), *Teaching arts and sciences with the new social media: Cutting-edge technologies in higher education* (vol. 3). Bingley, U.K.: Emerald Group.

Hernandez, C., Newman, P., & Lopez, R. (2014). *Facebook me: Using social media to promote college retention*. Retrieved from http://media.collegeboard.com

/digitalServices/pdf/diversity/2014/facebook-me-using-social-media-promote-college-retention.pdf.

Hewitt, A., & Forte, A. (2006). *Crossing boundaries: Identity management and student/faculty relationships on Facebook*. Poster presented at the Computer Supported Cooperative Work (CSCW).

Hoffman, E. (2009).Social media and learning environments: Shifting perspectives on the locus of control. *In Education: Exploring Our Connective Educational Landscape, 15*(2), 23-38. Retrieved from http://ined.uregina.ca/ineducation/article/view/54/0.

Huffman, S. (2013). Benefits and pitfalls: Simple guidelines for the use of social networking tools in K-12 education. *Education, 134*(2), 154-160.

Jones, A. (2011). How Twitter saved my literature class: A case study with discussion. In C. Wankel (Ed.), *Teaching arts and sciences with the new social media: Cutting-edge technologies in higher education* (vol. 3). Bingley, U.K.: Emerald Group.

Jones, J. G., Morales, C, & Knezek, G. A. (2005). 3-Dimensional online learning environments: examining attitudes toward information technology between students in Internet-based 3-dimensional and face-to-face classroom instruction. *Educational Media International, 42*(3), 219-36.

Journell, W., Ayers, C. A., & Beeson, M. W. (2014). Tweeting in the classroom. *Phi Delta Kappan, 95*(5), 63.

Junco, R. (2011). *Twitter to improve college student engagement*. Paper presented at SXSW Interactive, Austin, Texas, 2011.

Junco, R. (2012). The relationship between frequency of Facebook use, participation in Facebook activities, and student engagement. *Computers & Education, 58*, 162-171. doi:10.1016/j.compedu.2011.08.004.

Junco, R., Heiberger, G., & Loken, E. (2011). The effect of Twitter on college student engagement and grades. *Journal of Computer Assisted Learning, 27*(2), 119–132. doi:10.1111/j.1365-2729.2010.00387.x.

Keengwe, J., Kidd, T., & Kyei-Blankson, L. (2009). Faculty and technology: Implications for faculty training and technology leadership. *Journal of Science Education Technology, 18*, 23-28.

Lemoine, P., & Richardson, M. D. (2013). Cyberlearning: The impact of instruction on higher education. *The Researcher: An Interdisciplinary Journal, 26*, 57-83.

Lepi, K. (2013). *How social media is being used in education*. Retrieved from http://www.edudemic.com/social-media-in-education/.

Liu, M., Kalk, D., Kinney, L., & Orr, G. (2009). Web 2.0 and its use in higher education: A review of literature. World Conference on E-learning in Corporate, Government, Healthcare, and Higher Education (ELEARN), October 26.

Liu, Z. F., & Chang, Y. F. (2010). Gender differences in usage, satisfaction, and performance of blogging. *British Journal of Education Technology, 41*, 39-43. doi:10.1111/j.1467-8535.2009.00939.x.

Long, C. (2009, June 18). *Online social networking for educators: Educators build community and collaboration online*. http://wsww.nea.org/hem/20746.htm.

Mao, J. (2014). Social media for learning: A mixed methods study on high school students' technology affordances and perspectives. *Computers in Human Behavior, 33*, 213-223. doi:10.1016/j.chb.2014.01.002.

Martindale, T., & Dowdy, M. (2010). Personal learning environments. In G. Veletsianos (Ed.), *Emerging technologies in distance education* (pp. 177–193). Edmonton, AB: Athabasca University Press.

Mazer, J. P., Murphy, R. E., & Simonds, C. J. (2007). I'll see you on "Facebook." The effects of computer-mediated teacher self-disclosure on student motivation, affective learning, and classroom climate. *Communication Education, 56*, 1-17. doi:10.1080/03634520601009710.

McClure, A. (2013). *Social media for retention: Missed opportunities*. Retrieved from http://www.universitybusiness.com/article/social-media-retention-are-colleges-missing-opportunities.

McEwan, B. (2012). Managing boundaries in the Web 2.0 classroom. *New Directions for Teaching & Learning, 131,* 15-28. doi:10.1002/tl.20024.

Mishra, T., Lemoine, P., Campbell, K., Mense, E. G., & Richardson, M. D. (2013). Social media and instruction: Irreconcilable differences? In H. H. Yang, Z. Yang, D. Wu, & S. Liu (Eds.), *Transforming K-12 classrooms with digital technology.* Hershey, PA.: IGI.

National Science Foundation (2008). *Fostering learning in the networked world: The cyberlearning opportunity and challenge. A 21st century agenda for the National Science Foundation.* Arlington, VA: The National Science Foundation. Retrieved from: http://www.nsf.gov/pubs/2008/nsfD82O4/nsf082O4_1.pdf.

Newmann, F. M., & Wehlage, G. G. (1993). Five standards of authentic instruction. *Educational Leadership, 50,* 8-12.

Nicolini, D., Mengis, J., & Swan, J. (2012). Understanding the role of objects in crossdisciplinary collaboration. *Organization Science, 23*(3), 612-629. doi:10.1287/orsc.1110 .0664.

Pascarella, E. T. (1985). Students' affective development within the college environment. *Journal of Higher Education, 56,* 640-663.

Puzio, E. (2013). Why can't we be friends? How far can the state go in restricting social networking communications between secondary school teachers and their students? *Cardozo Law Review, 34*(3), 1099-1127.

O'Reilly, T., & Battelle, J. (2009). *Web squared: Web 2.0 five years on.* Special report for the Web 2.0 summit. San Francisco CA. Retrieved from http://assets.en.oreilly.com/1 /event/28/web2009_websquared-whitepaper.pdf.

Queirolo, J. (2009). Is Facebook as good as face-to-face? *Learning and Leading with Technology, 57*(4), 8-9.

Ramig, R. (2014). *One-to-one computing and learning: Has it lived up to its expectations?* Retrieved from http://www.internetatschools.com/Articles/Editorial/Features/One -to-One-Computing-and-Learning-Has-It-Lived-Up-to-Its-Expectations-95178.aspx.

Roorda, D. L., Koomen, H. M. Y., Spilt, J. L., & Oort, F. J. (2011). The influence of affective teacher-student relationships on students' school engagement and achievement: A meta-analytical approach. *Review of Educational Research, 81,* 493-529. doi:10.3102/0034654311421793.

Schirmer, J. (2011). Fostering meaning and community in writing course via social media. In C. Wankel (ed.), *Teaching arts and sciences with the new social media: Cutting-edge technologies in higher education* (vol. 3). Bingley, U.K.: Emerald Group.

Schwartz, H. L. (2009). Facebook: The new classroom commons? *Chronicle of Higher Education, 56*(6), B12–13.

Sharples, M., Graber, R., Harrison, C., & Logant, K. (2008). E-safety and Web 2.0 for children aged 11–16. *Journal of Computer Assisted Learning, 25,* 70–84.

Sheldon, P. (2014). *Applying the theory of reasoned action to student-teacher relationships on Facebook.* Paper presented at the annual meeting of the Association for Education in Journalism and Mass Communication (AEJMC), Montreal, Canada.

Shih, C, & Waugh, M. (2011). Web 2.0 Tools for learning in higher education: The presence of blogs, wikis, podcasts, microblogs, Facebook and Ning. In M. Koehler and P. Mishra (Eds.), *Proceedings of Society for Information Technology and Teacher Education International Conference 2011* (pp. 3345-52). Chesapeake, VA: AACE.

Sim, J. W. S., & Hew, K. F. (2010). The use of weblogs in higher education settings: A review of empirical research. *Educational Research Review, 5*(2), 151–163. doi:10.1016 /j.edurev.2010.01.001.

Social admissions report (2013). Retrieved from http://www.theslateonline.com/article /2013/11/su-uses-social-media-to-attract-new-students.

Sturgeon, C. M., & Walker, C. (2009). *Faculty on Facebook: Confirm or deny.* Paper presented at the Annual Instructional Technology Conference, Murfreesboro, TN.

Thompson, C., Gray, K., & Kim, H. (2014). How social are social media technologies (SMTs)? A linguistic analysis of university students' experiences of using SMTs for learning. *Internet & Higher Education, 21,* 31-40. doi:10.1016/j.iheduc.2013.12.001.

Thompson, D. (2014, June 19). *The most popular social network for young people? Texting.* Retrieved from http://www.theatlantic.com/technology/archive/2014/06/facebook-texting-teens-instagram-snapchat-most-popular-social-network/373043/.

Van Merriënboer, J. J. G., & Stoyanov, S. (2008). Learners in a changing learning landscape: Reflections from an instructional design perspective. In J. Visser & M. Visser-Valfrey (Eds.), *Learners in a changing learning landscape* (pp. 69-90). New York: Springer.

Xie, Y., Ke, F., & Sharma, P. (2008). The effect of peer feedback for blogging on college students' reflective learning processes. *The Internet and Higher Education, 11*(4), 18-25.

Yang, C., & Chang, Y. (2011). Assessing the effects of interactive blogging on student attitudes towards peer interaction, learning motivation, and academic achievements. *Journal of Computer Assisted Learning, 28*(2), 126-135. doi:10.1111/j.1365-2729.2011.00423.x.

SEVEN

Social Media and Disaster Communication

Natural disasters are not a new thing; however, with the emergence of social media, things have changed as the entire world can learn about them in a matter of seconds. Ordinary people use social media to spread news and raise money; rescue and relief workers communicate with one another and with citizens who need help; the displaced are reaching out to their family and friends. For many, social media such as Facebook, YouTube and Twitter provide the latest developments during and after a disaster. Social media have the potential to get a message out quickly to anywhere in the world. The Federal Emergency Management Agency urges citizens to let their loved ones know that they are okay by sending a tweet or by updating their Facebook status. Social media strategist Mari Smith says that we now have social disasters, social emergencies, social earthquakes, and social hurricanes (DiBlasio, 2012). Social media have a viral potential as people share their videos taken by smartphones on social network sites.

Social media can help save people's lives. The 2010 Haiti earthquake brought about the idea of real-time "crisis mapping," allowing relief workers to locate those who needed help. While compassion knows no boundaries, a digital divide still exists in some countries where smartphones are few and the Internet is not affordable or available. In Haiti, many people still relied on radio and word of mouth for news. Where available, victims have reached to social media to communicate with loved ones after a disaster.

DEFINITION OF A DISASTER

A disaster is a "serious disruption of the functioning of a community or a society causing widespread human, material, economic, or environmental losses which exceed the ability of the affected community or society to cope using its own resources" (National Science and Technology Council, 2005, p. 21). According to the National Consortium for the Study of Terrorism and Responses to Terrorism (2012), disaster communication deals with (1) disaster information disseminated to the public by government and emergency management organizations via traditional or social media; (2) disaster information created and shared by journalists and the affected public, often through word of mouth and social media. Unlike disasters that are community-based and often uncontrollable, crises are organization-based and often man-made (Seeger, Sellnow, & Ulmer, 1998). A crisis is defined as "an event, which is often sudden or unexpected, that disrupts the normal operations of the institution or its educational mission and threatens the well-being of personnel, property, financial resources, and/or reputation of the institution" (Zdziarski, 2006, p. 5). For example, while floods and earthquakes are classified as natural disasters, a shooting is a crisis. In this chapter the terms are used interchangeably as a natural disaster can lead to a crisis.

SOCIAL MEDIA IN DISASTER COMMUNICATION

Social media are an increasingly important component of disaster communication (Howell & Taylor, 2012). According to an American Red Cross study (2010), one in six people from the general population uses social media to get information on a disaster. The terrorist attacks on 9/11 showed the need for advanced technology in communicating in a disaster situation (Freberg, Saling, Vidoloff, & Eosco, 2013). When US Airways Flight 1549 splashed into the Hudson River in 2009, Twitter was the first medium to publish the photo (Baron & Philbin, 2009). Twitter was one of the first sources of eyewitness information during the Mumbai terror attack in 2008 (Burg-Brown & Mistick, 2012) and the 2007 California wildfires (Veil, Buehner, & Palenchar, 2011). After the 2010 Haiti earthquake, text messages and social media were critical resources employed in rescue efforts (Burg-Brown & Mistick, 2012), although many people did not have Internet access. Responding to social media appeals, smartphone users raised $25 million for the Red Cross in ten days by texting "Haiti" to 90999 and adding $10 to their phone bills. When an earthquake and tsunami hit Japan in 2011, people used blogs for emotional release and support, logged onto Twitter to find and distribute breaking news, and watched YouTube videos to view and share shocking disaster visuals (PEJ New Media Index, 2011). After the earthquake, a Japanese Twitter user reached out to the American ambassador in Japan, John Roos, with the following tweet: "Kameda hospital in Chiba needs to transfer 80 patients from Kyoritsu hospital in Iwaki city, just outside of 30km (sic) range" (Abbasi, Kumar, Filho, & Liu 2012).

2011 Hurricane Irene was the first U.S. disaster where the official sources used social media to disseminate information about the disaster and preparation (Abbasi et al., 2012). 1.1 million tweets mentioned the word "hurricane" during Hurricane Sandy in 2012. Sandy became the second most talked about topic on Facebook in 2012. Even before the popularity of social network sites, people were using other types of social media to either get information or to discuss a disaster. During the September 11, 2001 terrorist attacks, blogs were a popular place for people to discuss the attack (Orlando, 2010). After Hurricane Katrina in 2005, people established blogs and databases to gather whereabouts of missing individuals. One of the databases was PeopleFinder. PeopleFinder had two buttons: "I'm Looking for Someone" and "I Have Information about Someone."

Twenty minutes after the Virginia Tech shooting in 2007, a Facebook page appeared: "I'm OK at VT." Only 90 minutes after the event, a Wikipedia webpage was created that accurately described the massacre. During the Californian wildfires in 2007, people relied on text messages and social media to share the information. After the Haitian earthquake, crisis camps created OpenStreetMap software that took the Google map of the affected areas, and, using post-disaster satellite images, coded the damaged buildings and other critical information needed for rescuers.

According to the National Consortium for the Study of Terrorism and Responses to Terrorism (2012), the public uses social media during disasters for the following reasons:

- Convenience (everybody owns a smartphone)
- Social norms (friends and family are using it)
- Personal recommendations from friends
- Humor (humor as a coping mechanism)
- Information seeking
- Timely information
- Unique information
- Unfiltered information
- To determine the disaster's magnitude
- To check in with family and friends
- To self-mobilize
- To maintain a sense of community
- To seek emotional support and healing

Austin, Fisher Liu, and Jin (2012) studied how audiences seek information from social and traditional media sources, and the types of factors that affect media use during crises. Using the social-mediated crisis communication (SMCC) model, results revealed that audiences use social media during crises for insider information and to check in with family and friends, while they use traditional media for educational purposes. However, the overwhelming drive or motive for using social media is the sense of community. After the 2011 Japan earthquake, use of social media was associated with a positive psychological response and a sense of connectedness (Howell & Taylor, 2012). In reading the postings of others, respondents were encouraged by the help and support offered. They were no longer victims or bystanders. Howell and Taylor argued that social media is an avenue to engage with and monitor events or community opinion, unfiltered by mainstream media. Social media is timely, highly responsive, and an effective form of "virtual" psychological first aid that provides information, connectedness, help, and compassion to those affected (Howell & Taylor, 2012).

Another reason for using social media during crises is the unavailability of other channels of communication. Cho and Park (2013) explored social media use during Japan's 2011 earthquake. Immediately after the earthquake, landline and mobile phones were unavailable and people had to rely on social media. In fact, Twitter broke the news about the earthquake more quickly than traditional media. Cho and Park (2013), therefore, argued that during a crisis social media users are more likely to rely on peer-to-peer communication and information-oriented websites than on official media sources. They also found that during a crisis Twitter users post less self-oriented posts and focus on providing crisis-related information instead. When a disaster happens, the number of replies on Twitter actually decreases, while the number of re-tweets increases (Cho & Park, 2013).

During natural disasters people use social media to find or report a missing person, as well as to request supplies and help in rebuilding the impacted region. For example, the Google Person Finder was created in response to the 2010 Haiti earthquake to help people reconnect with friends and loved ones in the aftermath of natural and humanitarian disasters. The site was used during the 2010 Chile earthquake, the 2011 Tohoku earthquake and tsunami, as well as during the Boston Marathon bombings. In fact, during the 2013 Boston Marathon bombings, social media acted as both an emergency tool and as a platform to express grief (Bellantoni, 2013). Twitter was faster than radio and television in reporting what was happening at the marathon. Twitter had both actual photographs and witness testimonies, thus helping with the reporting as well as with the sense of community and sharing of sympathy.

Hjorth and Kim (2011) studied how effective social mobile media was in maintaining relationships in times of earthquake disasters in Japan. With mobile media and phone lines jammed, social media expanded on previous modes of civic engagement and media by providing various modes of visual, textual, and oral communication. Social media "allow(s) for a new sense of collective affective power that makes us feel more connected" (p. 553) and is "able to participate despite boundaries—linguistic, geographic, and temporal" (p. 554). While new media sources do not make revolutions happen, Hjorth and Kim (2011) argue that they change the way that we conceptualize and experience those events. This experience is somewhat similar to the media archetype. For example, text messages and Twitter posts resemble a postcard. "Post" means to transfer. In fact, an earthquake that hit Tokyo in 1923 brought about the hottest medium at the time—a postcard. The idea of a picture postcard was to inform the general public of what had happened in the city with actual visual images. Postcards migrated across different spaces and temporalities, changing many hands, just like social media. The only difference was in the postcards not being immediate. During disasters, people use social media—which then function as some new type of networked counseling—but also as Hjorth and Kim (2011) argued, they highlighted the need for older media forms, including face-to-face.

Lachlan, Spence, and Lin (2014) focused on the social media website Twitter and the landfall of Hurricane Sandy by conducting a content analysis of the tweets preceding the event. These researchers maintain that Twitter is an efficient source of news and other information, such as the needs of victims, during a crisis (Lachlan, Spence, & Lin, 2014). Like other social network sites, Twitter is often a means for people to connect with others during times of duress and uncertainty. Using this medium during crisis communication may work to counteract these negative feelings for the victims, their loved ones, and other concerned citizens. Furthermore, Wasike (2013) notes that Twitter may use framing techniques that traditional media sources often use. This consists of promoting human interests, conflict, and economic interest elements of news, while other social network sites use these methods less frequently.

CHANNEL COMPLEMENTARITY AND MEDIA DEPENDENCY THEORY

According to *channel complementarity theory* (Dutta-Bergman, 2006), audiences select certain types of media based upon the function relevant to them. These forms of media tend to match audiences' perceptions and ways of thinking that reinforce their beliefs. Ryan (2013) argued that the type of disaster determines how people seek information. Different media sources serve different functions during disasters. Juric and Sylvester (2007) reported the results of surveys and focus groups with American and international students in order to explain the differences in media usage following Hurricane Katrina in 2005. Their results showed that most people relied on television first (visual, dramatic footage; people want to see the photos of damage), followed by the Internet (can specify a keyword and avoid repetitive TV coverage). A battery-powered radio was used only if the power was lost for those directly affected by the disaster. Juric and Sylvester (2007) argued that, during a disaster, the media-audience relationship changes as well. It becomes more intense, providing not just the needed information, but emotional support and a sense of community as well. According to *media dependency theory* (Ball-Rokeach & DeFleur, 1976), the overall dependency relationship between individuals and media content is stronger when exposure to the media is higher. It is also stronger if media outlets can satisfy more of the audiences' needs. Media dependency theory argues that we become dependent on media that meet a number of our needs. It is our familiarity with the media that makes us more dependent on it during natural disasters.

Social media is a popular choice for during and after a disaster, as they possess characteristics of participation, openness, conversation, community, and connectedness (Mayfield, 2006). Through social media, the news of crises can be shared and re-shared reaching millions of people without the presence of journalists. However, embracing social media does not mean discontinuing the use of mainstream media. These two sources can complement one another (Wright & Hinson, 2009). Following TV news, most people turned to Facebook as the second key source of information during Australian flooding in 2011, as well as during the 2011 Japanese earthquake (Howell & Taylor, 2012). Practitioners should not neglect traditional media in a crisis response. They should also not neglect word-of-mouth communication. In Austin, Fisher Liu, and Jin's study (2012), interviews indicated that people hear about a crisis through word of mouth first, then TV, and finally Facebook. Traditional media also had a higher perception of credibility.

How individuals use and interact with social media sources during disasters can be monitored by measuring social media usage. According to the SMCC model (Jin & Liu, 2010), there are three types of groups who produce and consume information before, during, and after crises: a) influential social media creators who create crisis information for others to consume, b) social media followers who consume it, and c) social media inactives who consume through word of mouth from followers or creators. The majority of those active on social media during disasters are followers (b) (Austin, Fisher Liu, & Jin, 2012).

FRAMING THE CRISIS MESSAGE

Several studies (e.g., Schultz, Utz, & Goritz, 2011; Cho & Gower, 2006) have found that during a disaster, the medium matters more than the message. The public perceives not the objective facts of a crisis situation, but by what construct that media or the news releases them. In other words, how the media describes the crisis may influence the public's perception of it. A human interest frame, for example, makes people regard the crisis as serious, urgent, or dangerous. Journalists often use the quote "If it bleeds, it leads." In a Cho and Gower (2006) study, a group that was exposed to a story with a human interest frame showed a significantly stronger emotional response than a group that was not exposed to that frame. Cho and Gower argued that over-dramatized coverage, a hysterical journalism, stimulates the psychological pulse and affects people's perceptions more negatively toward parties concerned with the event.

Westerman, Spence, and Lachlan (2009) argued that fascination with threatening news is a measure of self-protection. News stories covering disasters draw attention. Increased fear from a news story produces increased attention to that story (Young, 2003). According to exemplification theory (Zillmann, 2002), exemplars that are concrete, iconic, and emotionally arousing influence perceptions of issues more than abstract, symbolic, and emotionally inconsequential exemplars. Exemplification motivates people to take a protective action in response to this increased threat. Those who are personally involved in a disaster will also be more interested in the social media news. Past research (Choi & Lin, 2009b; MacInnis, Rao, & Weiss, 2002; Claeys & Cauberghe, 2013) has found that individuals with high crisis involvement scrutinize crisis information more in depth than those who are low in involvement.

MEDIA CREDIBILITY DURING CRISES

During disasters, people seek immediate and accurate information on social media (Bates & Callison, 2008). The first reports of the 2008 earthquake in China came from Twitter (Mills, Chen, Lee, & Rao, 2009). According to a survey of residents affected by the southern California wildfires in 2007, many felt that the mainstream media did not provide enough information in a timely manner. In response, citizens turned to social media for information (Mills, et al., 2009).

Lachlan, Spence, Edwards, Reno, and Edwards (2014) investigated the perceived trustworthiness of social media messages on the basis of the speed of the updates. Researchers argue that if someone repeatedly seeks out particular sources or media for information, they will grow to trust them. In terms of social media sites, by default consistent and timely updates will promote information-seeking behaviors. In line with the researchers' argument, this would demonstrate trust and perceived credibility, so the perceived risk should be based on the trustworthiness of the source and/or the medium. The judgment of the severity of the social media message and its credibility are very important because they will determine the behavior of the message's recipient. If the message is a warning of some sort, these factors may affect whether safety precautions are followed, whether the information is spread, how it is spread, and to whom. This is of particular importance to colleges and universities that have adapted emergency procedures to include widespread calls, text message alerts, e-mails, and social media updates. However, very few studies have explored how technology choices influence the perception of the seriousness of a crisis event. Sheldon (2015) explored how technology channels (text message vs. social medium) used to alert students about a campus crisis (mass shooting vs. tornado) affect students' perception of the seriousness of the event, their intention to share the received information with parents and friends, and the preferred channel to do so. A study was conducted with 177 college students, and the results revealed that an alert about the crisis that the university sends through text message is perceived to be more serious than an alert sent through Facebook. Regardless of the medium of alert and crisis type, the first person students said they would notify would be someone sitting nearby. In line with other media dependency studies, it is our familiarity with the media that makes us more dependent on it during disasters.

SOCIAL MEDIA DEFICIENCIES

According to the National Consortium for the Study of Terrorism and Responses to Terrorism (2012), the reasons that the public might not use social media during a disaster include:

- Privacy and security fears
- Accuracy concerns
- Access issues (power outages; digital divide)
- Knowledge deficiencies

During a large-scale disaster, the incident is initially reported by a local eyewitness with a cell phone device, and is then distributed through social media services, followed by the mainstream media (Oh, Agrawal, & Rao, 2011). Oh et al. argue that online citizens have the potential of being first responders as they possess local knowledge typically not available to professional emergency responders living outside of the affected community. This, however, can contribute to collective rumor mills, misinformation, and gossip. Large-scale social crises often lead to information overload, including inaccurate reports. Oh, Agrawal, and Rao (2013) argued that one important task for crisis response is to control rumors and obtain local and reliable information to the affected communities as soon as possible through multiple communication channels.

GUIDELINES FOR PR PRACTITIONERS

An increasing number of public relations practitioners are using social media platforms to gauge sentiments of their publics, prevent crises, or cope with crisis. Howell and Taylor argued that crisis managers need to establish guidelines on how to use the new communication tools. A crisis plan is incomplete without a comprehensive digital strategy (Howell & Taylor, 2012). The mainstream media also use Facebook pages as a source of information for news stories and updates. In order to develop trust-based relationships, official sites must be established before the disaster strikes (Howell & Taylor, 2012). According to FEMA's (2012) Social Media for Natural Disaster Response and Recovery guidelines, social media are used in disaster management to prepare the public for emergencies, to monitor for help needed, to alert and warn the public, for relief and recovery efforts, data collection, and to keep the public updated with news and information. Social media should be used in both the preparedness/mitigation, response, and recovery phases. A Red Cross survey (2010) revealed that the public expects disaster organizations to use social media. One of the duties of such organizations is to monitor and respond to emergency requests, as 74 percent of people expect help to arrive within an hour (American Red Cross, 2010). FEMA (2012) guidelines urge disaster organizations to keep social media messages "brief and pertinent" following the "one voice, multiple channel" principle. However, depending on the objectives, different platforms might be more useful than others. While Twitter is faster and more appropriate for brief news and updates, the structure of Facebook encouraged more community building and discussion (FEMA, 2012). Although some organizations have created a regular Facebook profile, FEMA encourages everybody to create a Facebook page. Unlike a profile which is private, a Facebook page is public and people can "like" it without actually becoming official Facebook friends.

Arizona State University researchers (Abbasi et al., 2012) have developed a Twitter monitoring and analysis system—TweetTracker—that can easily track and retrieve disaster-related information to assist first respondents to make effective decisions. Abbasi et al. (2012) have tested the system using a live-action role-playing exercise in which game victims use social media to ask for help. These requests are then processed by a relief system (TweetTracker) that generates a report for first responders to use. Based on a simulated game, Abbasi and colleagues offered several lessons. The first one is to collect the related tweets. A proper method has to be employed in order to screen millions and millions of tweets. Second, people need to learn to share their location in a tweet (geolocation). Due to privacy concerns and the lack of awareness about this feature, less than 5 percent of users provide location information with their tweets (Abbasi et al., 2012).

Orlando (2010) argued that social media are not a channel for pushing information out to the public. They involve pulling information and resources from the public. Orlando further urges business communities to use social media. Collaborative knowledge can be much more accurate than that from a single source. People will talk about the event with or without the official sources (Orlando, 2010).

Page, Freberg, and Saling (2013) urged crisis management, including government agencies, to use social media in preparation for a crisis, not just the response and recovery phases. Preparation includes creating a crisis plan and refining a communication system to use all forms of media. Page et al. argued that how emergency respondents and community officials provide timely and accurate information during crises is still an unexplored research area. Preparing a crisis plan can help reduce the public's fear and uncertainty, as well as enhance the credibility of responders.

Freberg, Saling, Vidoloff, and Eosco (2013) developed the Emerging Media Crisis Value Model (EMCV) explaining general functions and subfunctions of a crisis message. The value messages include: communicate quickly, be credible, be accurate, be simple, be complete, and communicate broadly. However, the "be credible" value message does not apply to acts of nature, such as hurricanes. The model identified the three best practices for the use of social media in a crisis: a) integration of multimedia and links into updates, b) proper use of hashtags and tagged keywords, and c) balance between official and conversational updates.

Page et al. (2013) used the EMCV model to define what constitutes a "good" crisis message. They analyzed two cases: Hurricane Irene, which hit the East Coast of the United States during the hurricane season of 2011, and also the Aurora, Colorado theater shooting that happened in 2012 when a lone gunman named James Holmes entered the theater armed after midnight and killed 12 people. Page et al. (2013) found that when comparing a natural disaster crisis communication to communication during a man-made crisis, all of the value measures remain the same except the attribution of responsibility. In a man-made crisis, the public is looking for a responsible party, as that crisis could have been prevented. Based on their results, Page et al. (2013) recommend the use of visual social platforms such as Instagram, Pinterest, and Tumblr, as those are becoming more popular than text-based forms. For example, FEMA has an active social media presence even when there are no serious crises going on in the United States. On its Facebook page, FEMA regularly posts about how to prepare for a disaster. It relies on videos and photographs to inform and teach people about the importance of taking safety measures before anything occurs. Overall, social media are valuable in all phases of a disaster, and many social media tools can be used simultaneously (FEMA, 2012).

REFERENCES

Abassi, M. A., Kumar, S., Filho, J. A. A, & Liu, H. (2012). *Lessons learned in using social media for disaster relief—ASU crisis response game.* In SBP's 12 Proceedings of the 5th International Conference on Social Computing, Behavioral-Cultural Modeling and Prediction, p. 282-289.

American Red Cross (2010). *Social media in disasters and emergencies.* American Red Cross, Washington, DC.

Austin, L., Fisher Liu, B., & Jin, Y. (2012). How audiences seek out crisis information: Exploring the social-mediated crisis communication model. *Journal of Applied Communication Research, 40,* 188-207. doi:10.1080/00909882.2012.654498.

Ball-Rokeach, S. J., & DeFleur, M. L. (1976). A dependency model of mass media effects. *Communication Research, 3,* 3-21. doi:10.1177/009365027600300101.

Baron, G. & Philbin, J. (2009). Social media in crisis communication: Start with a drill. *Public Relations Tactics, 16*(4), 12.

Bates, L., & Callison, C. (2008). *Effect of company affiliation on credibility in the blogosphere.* Paper presented at the Association for Education in Journalism and Mass Communication Conference, Chicago, IL.

Bellantoni, C. (2013). *In face of disaster, social media helped spread news and connect Bostonians.* Retrieved from http://www.pbs.org/newshour/bb/media/jan-june13/dd_04-16.html.

Burg-Brown, S., & Mistick, D. (2012). One question, two members. *Journal of Property Management, 77*(5), 9.

Cho, S. E., & Park, H. W. (2013). Social media use during Japan's 2011 earthquake: How Twitter transforms the locus of crisis communication. *Media International Australia, 149,* 28-40.

Cho, S., & Gower, K. K. (2006). Framing effect on the public's response to crisis: Human interest frame and crisis type influencing responsibility and blame. *Public Relations Review, 32*(4), 420-422. doi:10.1016/j.pubrev.2006.09.011.

Choi, Y., & Lin, Y-H. (2009a). Consumer responses to Mattel product recalls posted on online bulletin boards: Exploring two types of emotion. *Journal of Public Relations Research, 21*(2), 198-207. doi:10.1080/10627260802557506.

Choi, Y., & Lin, Y. -H. (2009b). Consumer response to crisis: Exploring the concept of involvement in Mattel product recalls. *Public Relations Review, 35*(1), 18-22. doi:10.1016/j.pubrev.2008.09.009.

Claeys, A.-S., & Cauberghe, V. (2013). What makes crisis response strategies work? The impact of crisis involvement and message framing. *Journal of Business Research, 67,* 182-189. doi:10.1016/j.jbusres.2012.10.005.

DiBlasio, N. (2012, August 30). Relief groups try tweets, apps to spread the news. *USA Today,* p 4A.

Dutta-Bergman, M. J. (2006). Community participation and Internet use after September 11: Complementarity in channel consumption. *Journal of Computer-Mediated Communication, 11,* 469-484. doi:10.1111/j.1083-6101.2006.00022.x.

FEMA (2012). Social media for natural disaster response and recovery. Retrieved from http://www.utc.edu/safety-risk-management/pdfs/website/conference/social-media-handouts.pdf.

Freberg, K., Saling, K., Vidoloff, K. G., & Eosco, G. (2013). Using value modeling to evaluate social media messages: The case of Hurricane Irene. *Public Relations Review, 39*(3), 185-192. doi:10.1016/j.pubrev.2013.02.010.

Hjorth, L., & Kim, K. (2011). The mourning after: A case study of social media in the 3.11 earthquake disaster in Japan. *Television & New Media, 12*(6), 552-559. doi:10.1177/1527476411418351.

Howell, G. V. J., & Taylor, M. (2012). *When a crisis happens, who turns to Facebook and why?* Retrieved from http://www.deakin.edu.au/arts-ed/apprj/articles/12-howell-taylor.pdf.

Jin, Y., & Liu, B. F. (2010). The blog-mediated crisis communication model: Recommendations for responding to influential external blogs. *Journal of Public Relations Research, 22*, 429-455. doi:10.1080/10627261003801420.

Juric, P., & Sylvester, J. (2007). Mass media use during a natural disaster: Louisiana State University students and Hurricane Katrina. *Southwestern Mass Communication Journal, 22*, 85-96.

Lachlan, K. A., Spence, P. R., Edwards, C., Reno, K., & Edwards, A. (2014). If you are quick enough, I'll think about it: Information speed and trust in public health organizations. *Computers in Human Behavior, 33*(2), 377-380.

Lachlan, K. A., Spence, P. R., & Lin, X. (2014). Expressions of risk awareness and concern through Twitter: On the utility of using the medium as an indication of audience needs. *Computers in Human Behavior, 35*, 554-559. doi:10.1016/j.chb.2014.02.029.

MacInnis, D. J., Rao, A., & Weiss, A. (2002). Assessing when increased media weight of real-world advertisements helps sales. *Journal of Marketing Research, 39*(4), 391–407. doi:http://dx.doi.org/10.1509/jmkr.39.4.391.19118.

Mayfield, A. (2006). *What is social media?* Spannerworks. Retrieved from http://www.spannerworks.com/fileadmin/uploads/eBooks/What_is_Social_Media.pdf.

Mills, A., Chen, R., Lee, J., & Rao, H. R. (2009). *Web 2.0 emergency applications: How useful can Twitter be for an emergency response?* Retrieved from http://denman-mills.net/web_documents/jips_mills.etal._2009.07.22_finalsubmission.pdf.

National Consortium for the Study of Terrorism and Responses to Terrorism (2012). *Social media use during disasters: A review of the knowledge base and gaps.* Retrieved from http://www.start.umd.edu/sites/default/files/files/publications/START_SocialMediaUseduringDisasters_LitReview.pdf.

National Science and Technology Council (2005, June). *Grand challenge for disaster reduction: A report of the Subcommittee on Disaster Reduction.* Washington, D.C.: National Science and Technology Council, Executive Office of the President, Washington, D.C. Retrieved from http://www.nehrp.gov/pdf/grandchallenges.pdf.

Oh, O., Agrawal, M., & Rao, H. R. (2011). Information control and terrorism: Tracking the Mumbai terrorist attack through Twitter. *Information Systems Frontier, 13*, 33-44.

Oh, O., Agrawal, M., & Rao, H. R. (2013). Community intelligence and social media services: A rumor theoretic analysis of tweets during social crises. *MIS Quarterly, 37*, 407-426.

Orlando, J. (2010). Harnessing the power of social media in disaster response. *Continuity Insights.* Retrieved from http://www.continuityinsights.com/articles/2010/09/harnessing-power-social-media-disaster-response.

Page, S., Freberg, K., & Saling, K. (2013). Emerging media crisis value model: A comparison of relevant, timely message strategies for emergency events. *Journal of Strategic Security, 6*, 20-31. doi:10.5038/1944-0472.6.2.2.

PEJ New Media Index (2011, March 14-18). In social media it's all about Japan. *Pew Research Center's Project for Excellence in Journalism.* Retrieved from http://www.journalism.org/2011/03/24/social-media-its-all-about-japan/.

Ryan, B. (2013). Information seeking in a flood. *Disaster Prevention and Management, 22*, 229-242.

Schultz, F., Utz, S., & Goritz, A. (2011). Is the medium the message? Perceptions of and reactions to crisis communication via Twitter, blogs and traditional media. *Public Relations Review, 37*(1), 20-27. doi:10.1016/j.pubrev.2010.12.001.

Seeger, M. W., Sellnow, T. L., & Ulmer, R. R. (1998). Communication, organization, and crisis. *Communication Yearbook, 21*, 231-275.

Sheldon, P. (2015). *Alerting students about a crisis: Technology preferences and secondary crisis communication.* Presented at the International Communication Association conference, San Juan, Puerto Rico.

Veil, S. R., Buehner, T., & Palenchar, M. J. (2011). A work-in-process literature review: Incorporating social media in risk and crisis communication. *Journal of Contingencies and Crisis Management, 19*, 110-122. doi:10.1111/j.1468-5973.2011.00639.x.

Wasike, B. S. (2013). Framing News in 140 Characters: How Social Media Editors Frame the News and Interact with Audiences via Twitter. *Global Media Journal: Canadian Edition, 6*(1), 5-23.

Westerman, D., Spence, P. R., & Lachlan, K. A. (2009). Telepresence and the exemplification effects of disaster news. *Communication Studies, 60*, 542-557. doi:10.1080/10510970903260376.

Wright, D. K., & Hinson, M. D. (2009). *An analysis of the increasing impact of social and other new media on public relations practice.* International Public Relations Research Conference, Miami, FL. Retrieved from www.instituteforpr.org/wp-content/uploads/Wright_Hinson_PR_Miami.pdf.

Young, J. R. (2003). The role of fear in agenda setting by television news. *American Behavioral Scientist, 46*, 1673–1695. doi:10.1177/0002764203254622.

Zdziarski, E. L. (2006). Crisis in the context of higher education. In K. S. Harper, B. G. Paterson, & E. L. Zdziarski (Eds.), *Crisis management: Responding from the heart.* Washington, D.C.: National Association of Student Personnel Administrators.

Zillmann, D. (2002). Exemplification theory of media influence. In J. Bryant & D. Zillmann (Eds.), *Media effects: Advances in theory and research* (pp. 213–245). Mahwah, NJ: LEA.

EIGHT

Social Media and Advertising

The idea of social marketing is not new. However, in the last decade the Internet has been used to supplement traditional media in promoting products and services. Technology has changed the way individuals make buying decisions, conduct business, and interact with one another. Social network sites have removed the filters between the companies and the public, and have enabled a new way to communicate a company's brand identity. This chapter explores the pros and cons of advertising on social media sites, and further provides guidelines for how to advertise on Facebook, Twitter, YouTube, Pinterest, and LinkedIn.

ADVERTISING ON SOCIAL MEDIA

Communication between businesses and customers was revolutionized with the adoption of social media platforms, compared to the expensive standard online advertising (Megna, 2009). This trend coincides with the increase in online communities that provide a larger audience for a company's branding message to reach. From promoted posts and user-specific ads on Facebook, to trending brand topics and promoted tweets on Twitter, companies have a wide array of choices in how they reach out to current or potential customers. Because most people are using social media today, advertisers need to market to consumers on those sites.

While social media advertising is usually accompanied by traditional media advertising, three characteristics of social media have changed the advertising business. Those include interactivity, customization, and social interaction (Hill & Moran, 2011). *Interactivity* has been defined as "the degree to which a communication technology can create a mediated environment in which participants can communicate (one-to-one, one-to-many, and many-to-many), both synchronously and asynchronously, and participate in reciprocal message exchanges (third-order dependency)" (Kiousis, 2002, p. 372). Interactivity leads to a higher involvement (Bucy, 2003) and higher source credibility (Fogg, 2003). A brand or company's Facebook page is an example of how businesses can easily interact with customers. Emanuelli (2012) offered several suggestions for how to increase Facebook page interaction: engaging with the followers, sharing interesting content, sharing relevant news and articles, as well as using everyday language. For example, Nike's Facebook page uses a logo as the profile picture, and Nike's slogan "Just do it" on the cover page. This makes it easier for people to recognize the brand. Emanuelli (2012) also advises businesses to post personal images and videos. People like to see that the company is concerned about its people.

Another way to increase the confidence of an audience is to share the latest business achievements on a Facebook, Twitter, or LinkedIn page. Everybody likes to see that their preferred brand is doing well. Except for setting up its page, businesses can run traditional online display ads. Currently, Facebook is the most popular social network to advertise on. While most people say that they do not click on Facebook ads, the ads are still effective. In 2012, Facebook hired Datalogix to measure shopping habits of 100 million families to see if they purchase the product whose ad they saw on Facebook. The results showed that they do. In some cases, businesses were making three times more money in purchases than they had spent on the ad campaign (Manjoo, 2013).

Another characteristic of social media is customization. Customization includes treating customers and potential buyers differently based on the feedback from interaction (Peppers, Rogers, & Dorf, 1999). This helps the message credibility but also reduces costs by targeting certain segments instead of a mass audience. On Twitter, "tags" are used to facilitate searching based on interests (Hill & Moran, 2011). Twitter is a good choice for advertising to a niche audience. Facebook, on another hand, can reach the general public.

Finally, social media allow social interaction and constant interaction with friends and followers. Not only are individuals influenced by those whose opinions they value, but they can also be influenced by their virtual friends or followers. This is one big difference that separates it from traditional advertising. Social media allow for a two-way conversation between the marketer and the constituents, but they also allow constituents to talk to each other and be influenced by one another. A good example would be online rating services where anybody can review or recommend a product or a service.

Advantages

The advantages of advertising through social media include the cost, speed, reach, and two-way communication. First, advertising through social media is inexpensive. Most social media sites have free access. The cost to post an ad is much lower compared to other media types as well. This means that businesses can now reach their target audience for little or no cash investment. They can reach them at home, at remote locations, while also providing them with more information than would be possible through traditional forms of advertising.

In addition, advertising on social media is fast and easy. According to a recent report (Stelzner, 2014), 84 percent of marketers spent as little as six hours of effort per week updating their social media accounts. Some of the recommended strategies to improve the engagement include posting attention-grabbing quotes, using emoticons, question posts, giveaways and contests, humor and jokes, links to other useful content, using visual images, and interviews with staff members.

The viral nature of social media allow interesting ads to spread quickly among a large network of people (Weinberg, 2009). Viral advertising, or marketing buzz, is a very popular and easy way to promote a brand on social media. Users often share funny or unusual video clips, such as the Super Bowl's Puppy Love made by Budweiser. Another advantage of social media advertising includes the ability to target specific markets by reaching people who are most interested in what they have to offer. Consumers can complain on social media sites, and that helps the company to hear and respond to their grievances (Gommans, Krishnan, & Scheffold, 2001). Businesses thus have an advantage of immediately addressing the comment, apologizing publicly, and taking action to make it right. Companies can use social media to study what consumers are mostly interested in, and also what their behavioral patterns are.

Disadvantages

Advertising on social media is not without its cons. Problems include the issue of trust and privacy, trademark and copyright issues, as well as the ability of consumers to leave immediate negative feedback (Weinberg, 2009). In addition, updating social media with relevant content can be time consuming. Not every company has resources to employ a person who will monitor all the posts, respond to comments, and answer questions about the product while also being knowledgeable about them. In addition, consumers can leave negative feedback. Negative posts in social media have an effect five times higher than positive ones, according to researchers (Corstjens & Umblijs, 2012). Because most Internet firms collect a large amount of personal data from users and sell them to the advertisers, customers might resist personalized ads, viewing them as creepy and off-putting (Tucker, 2014).

HOW TO ADVERTISE ON SOCIAL MEDIA

Social media ads should be relevant and useful, but also friendly and engaging so that readers share it with their friends. Engagement is the key in social media advertising. For example, many restaurant businesses now use social media to receive feedback from customers. Feedback helps improve their business. Some businesses post photos of food that they are serving. Some night clubs publicize weekend or daylight specials on social media to get more traffic. Because consumers are always on social media (Powers, Advincula, Austin, & Graiko, 2013), reaching them directly through the site that they use to relax and talk to friends with is therefore very effective.

Another possibility is organizing contests and games with different prices and rewards. For example, users can post their photos on the timeline, and the owner of the photo that receives the most "likes" gets a prize. One thing that businesses cannot forget is that they have to be present on social media so people do not forget about them. Just like in a traditional advertising copy, statuses need to be short and interesting. They need to call for action. Statuses can also offer incentives and promote deals. For example, an ad for Hello Fresh on Facebook gives $30 off for any first-time buyers. However, it also includes a link to the Hello-Fresh.com website where they can order food.

Social media are a natural place for brand communities (Habibi, Laroche, & Richard, 2014). Brand communities are important because they have the potential to influence brand trust. The definition of a brand community emphasizes that it is a "specialized, non-geographically bound community based on a structured set of social relations among admirers of a brand" (Muniz & O'Guinn, 2001, p. 412). Those social relations include four relationships: customer-product, customer-brand, customer-company, and customer-other customers (Habibi et al., 2014). On Facebook, it is possible to target users who are not fan of the page yet, but have friends who are. This is an example of a customer-other customer relationship. Rating services are part of it as well. Because consumers interact with each other through these brand communities, they become stronger and also demand and expect more from the brands (Habibi et al., 2014).

Advertising through Facebook

With its dominant social networking reach online, Facebook is an essential online marketing tool for every business, big and small. According to Narayanan et al. (2012), Facebook provides three main features for companies: a dedicated page connected to their brand that allows current and potential customers to become "fans" by "liking" the brand's page; a social feature that allows specific posts to be promoted within its specific fan base, which is seen by the "friends" of the brand's fans; and, as previously mentioned, it also allows businesses to target specific audiences due to the accessibility of users' demographic information. Through a company's use of fan pages, promoted posts, and advertisements, targeted campaigns can include discounts, product or service coupons, and offline promotions. Commonly these incentives are offered only to "fans" of the page, which urges potential customers to click the "like" button and receive special offers.

Advertising through Twitter

Twitter is a bit different from Facebook when it comes to connecting with other users. The 140-character message, branded as a tweet, can be sent by any user and is displayed for all users who follow the user who "tweeted" the original message. With a feature listed as the "retweet" function, any other user—whether that user follows the original user or not—is able to "retweet" that original message, thus sending the message to that person's "following" list, also known as a timeline. The marketing use of Twitter is not only vital to having a crucial message sent out instantly, but it also allows companies to connect to its current and potential new customers. Twitter has the ability to reach a broad audience, often at a faster pace than Facebook, although its fanbase is smaller.

According to Twitter website, advertising on Twitter includes the following steps. First, businesses can select a campaign objective. Among the listed are those that help a company reach more people in terms of favorites, retweets, and replies, as well as engaging with the advertiser's mobile app. Second, advertisers can choose their target audience, based on geography, device, gender, and language, as well as by using keywords and people's interests. Twitter also has an Analytics service where they can learn more about their followers. According to its website, Twitter prohibits the advertising of alcohol content, financial services, gambling, health and pharmaceutical products and services, and political campaigning. In terms of advertising products, businesses have several options. They can choose a Promoted Account, which is priced on a Cost-per-Follow (CPF) basis, and the goal is to increase the number of followers on the Twitter profile. They can also choose to use the Promoted Tweet option, where tweets that are paid for appear in the timeline among those that are not paid. Ads are sold on an auction, which means that the tweet that gets promoted is the one with the highest bid. Only one Promoted tweet will appear on the user's timeline at any given time, and they are clearly identified as Promoted. The third possibility to advertise on Twitter includes Promoted Trends. Trending topics appear on the left side of the homepage and are also marked with a promoted icon. According to the Twitter website, Promoted Trends boost brand conversation.

Several studies have looked at Twitter ads' effectiveness. In 2012, Witkemper, Choong Hoon, and Waldburger studied how social media has changed the way consumers and fans have kept up with athletes. By examining motivations as to why one would keep up with an athlete, and a fan's constraints such as economic power and accessibility, Witkemper et al. were able to determine why certain athletes would be more marketable on Twitter than others. Their study found that the more followers a Twitter user has, the more likely people will see and interact with their tweets.

Hay (2010) examined the use of Twitter as a tool for tourism marketing by studying the current popularity of Twitter. Hay's study concluded that there are two questions that must be answered: can an organization, or a destination, be a friend on Twitter or social media, and who is actually listening when an organization, or an account that does not actually represent a person, tweets?

Advertising through YouTube

Because most people are visual learners, social media advertisers often take advantage of image and video-based platforms, such as YouTube and Pinterest. YouTube has advantages over television advertising as it reaches people even when they are not at home. It is a free platform, and most people use it when they are looking for specific content. Unlike television, YouTube videos are available 24/7 and can be reviewed multiple times.

Advertising on YouTube is simple and straightforward, and is managed through Google AdWords. Businesses can upload the video that they want to display and choose how much they want to spend on the campaign. They can choose their target audience based on demographics, topics, interests, and keywords. Through the Analytics tab in their YouTube account, advertisers can learn more about who their audience is, and through their AdWords account, they can track their views, clicks, and budget details. Other effective strategies include getting website owners to embed the videos on their websites, as well as sharing YouTube video on another social media site. Although one of the disadvantages of YouTube videos is the fact that viewers can skip watching it, YouTube ads are still quite effective.

Advertising through Pinterest

In 2014, Pinterest, another image-sharing social network site, announced the launching of paid ads. While retailers such as Dillards already had a "Pin It" button—which allowed the users to pin the image from their online website—the novelties are paid ads. Those paid ads are also called Promoted Pins. The idea for Promoted Pins is to look like normal pins, except for the "Promoted Pin" disclaimer at the bottom and the red border around the image to make it stand out from regular pins. At the time of writing this book, Pinterest was getting ready to launch an ad service. The cost of a Promoted Pin is supposed to be high compared to other social media, averaging $30 per impression (McDermott, 2014). It is then expected that big brands will take advantage of Pinterest, while it might be too expensive for local merchants to advertise. Ads are expected to be geared toward young female demographics, as those are the users on Pinterest. According to the pinterest.com website, an average Pin gets 11 repins.

Advertising through LinkedIn

Similar to other social media, LinkedIn allows businesses to promote themselves in several different ways. Those include Direct Sponsored Content and Sponsored Updates in the LinkedIn feed. Companies can create an ad featuring text, image, or video, as well as have existing or new content shared with the LinkedIn audience. Businesses can select a target audience by job title, job function, industry, geography, company name, and size. Depending on the company's budget, they can choose to pay only for the ads that get clicked through (cost per click, or CPC) or every time LinkedIn shows their ad (cost per 1,000 impressions). The lowest bid for the click is $2. Advertisers can also choose how long they want to run the campaign for. One of the advantages of advertising on LinkedIn includes the opportunity to target the right audience. For example, a law school that is looking to attract more students can target only individuals with the job title "legal assistant." They can not only target those occupations by the geographic location, but can also see the number of members with that specific title.

Viral Advertising

Viral advertising, or electronic word of mouth, is the "unpaid peer-to-peer communication of provocative content originating from an identified sponsor using the Internet to persuade or influence an audience to pass along the content to others" (Porter & Golan, 2006, p. 33). Viral advertising originated in the e-mail setting, but it gained popularity with social network sites. Studies have found that senders tend to experience positive emotions when they pass along the message to their friends or followers (Phelps, Lewis, Mobillo, Perry, & Raman, 2004). The most popular viral ads are viral video ads. Those ads are often clips that are first broadcast on television, such as Super Bowl ads (Dafonte-Gomez, 2013). Different analyses of the most successful viral video ads show that most of them contain an element of "surprise" (Dafonte-Gomez, 2013). Eckler and Bolls (2011) also argued that for videos to be shared, they have to generate emotions. In terms of the dissemination by users, the most successful video ads are those that contain sex and nudity-related content and are overall more dramatic than ads for television, as they are not subject to regulation by the Federal Communications Commission (Porter & Golan, 2006). In terms of length, Dafonte-Gomez (2013) found that viral video ads are not far from standard TV ads. However they are more effective, as consumers receive the information from more credible sources (their friends) than from advertisers (Nyilasy, 2004).

According to Narayanan et al. (2012), the idea of online marketing is to "target certain individuals in a network with promotional campaigns, and let them propagate the messages through the network." And usually centered in those promotional campaigns are individuals who bring with them a following, in Twitter terms. The more popular a certain individual is within a social network, the more influence that user has within his or her social community. This is a critical factor in terms of viral marketing, and these individuals are often the targets of certain campaigns, depending on the users' social communities.

SUMMARY

Overall, social media strategy should align with the businesses' marketing goals and target demographics. Not only do businesses have to be mindful of their posts, but they also need to monitor what people care about on social media, what trends they follow, what catches their eye. Thus, strategies have to be planned for social media just as they have to be planned for other types of media.

Advertising through social media outlets offers businesses a free platform to interact with current and potential consumers, to better understand their product needs, and offer specials related to their product. With the increased reliance on social media for entertainment and information, we could expect that social media advertising will further develop, allowing consumers to establish a more personal connection to advertisers and then virtually communicate with their friends and others about the products and services.

REFERENCES

Bucy, E. P. (2003). The interactivity paradox: Closer to the news but confused. In E. P. Bucy & J. E. Newhagen (Eds.), *Media access: Social and psychological dimensions of new technology use* (pp. 47-72). Mahwah, NJ: Erlbaum.

Corstjens, M., & Umblijs, A. (2012). The power of evil: The damage of negative social media strongly outweigh positive contributions. *Journal of Advertising Research*, 52(4), 433–449. doi:10.2501/JAR-52-4-433-449.

Dafonte-Gomez (2013). The key elements of viral advertising. From motivation to emotion in the most shared videos. *Comunicar*, 22(43), 199-206.

Eckler, P., & Bolls, P. (2011). Spreading the virus: Emotional tone of viral advertising and its effect on forwarding intention and attitudes. *Journal of Interactive Advertising, 11*, 1-11. doi:10.1080/15252019.2011.10722180.

Emanuelli, E. (2012). *How to increase interactivity on your Facebook fan page.* Retrieved from http://onlineincometeacher.com/socialmedia/increase-interactivity-on-face-book-fan-page/.

Fogg, B. J. (2003). *Persuasive technology: Using computers to change what we think and do.* Boston: Morgan Kaufmann.

Gommans, M., Krishnan, K.S. & Scheffold, K. B. (2001). From brand loyalty to e-loyalty: A conceptual framework. *Journal of Economic and Social Research, 3*, 43-58. doi:10.1.1.105.3103.

Habibi, M. R., Laroche, M., & Richard, M.-O. (2014). The roles of brand community and community engagement in building brand trust on social media. *Computers in Human Behavior, 37*, 152-161. doi:10.1016/j.chb.2014.04.016.

Hay, B. (2010). *Twitter Twitter - but who is listening? A review of the current and potential use of twittering as a tourism marketing tool.* Presented at the CAUTHE 2010 20th International Research Conference.

Hill, R. P., & Moran, N. (2011). Social marketing meets interactive media: Lessons for the advertising community. *International Journal of Advertising, 30*(5), 815-838. doi:10.2501/IJA-30-5-815-838.

Kiousis, S. (2002). Interactivity: A concept explication. *New Media & Society, 4*(3), 355-383. doi:10.1177/146144402320564392.

Manjoo, F. (2013). *Facebook followed you to the supermarket.* Retrieved from http://www.slate.com/articles/technology/technology/2013/03/facebook_advertisement_studies_their_ads_are_more_like_tv_ads_than_google.2.html.

McDermott, J. (2014). *How Pinterest is selling ads to agencies.* Retrieved from http://digiday.com/platforms/heres-pinterest-pitching-agencies-ads/.

Megna, M. (2009). *Facebook, Twitter, and social media marketing.* Retrieved from http://www.internetnews.com/ecnews/article.php/3839521/Facebookpercent2BTwitterpercent2Bandpercent2BSocialpercent2BMediapercent2BMarketing.htm.

Muniz, A. M., & O'Guinn, T. C. (2001). Brand community. *Journal of Consumer Research, 27*(4), 412–432. doi:10.1086/319618.

Narayanan, M., Asur, S., Nair, A., Rao, S., Kaushik, A., Mehta, D., Athalye, S. & Lalwani, R. (2012). Social media and business. *Vikalpa: The Journal for Decision Makers, 37*(4), 69-111.

Nyilasy, G. (2004). *Word-of-mouth advertising: A 50-year review and two theoretical models for an online chatting context.* Paper presented at the 2004 Convention of the Association for Education in Journalism and Mass Communication, Toronto, Canada.

Peppers, D., Rogers, M. & Dorf, R. (1999). Is your company ready for one-to-one marketing. *Harvard Business Review, 77*, 151–60.

Phelps, J. E., Lewis, R., Mobillo, L., Perry, D., & Raman, N. (2004). Viral marketing or electronic word-of-mouth advertising: Examining consumer responses and motivations to pass along email. *Journal of Advertising Research, 44*, 333-48. doi:10.1017/S0021849904040371.

Porter, L., & Golan, G. (2006). From subservient chickens to brawny men: A comparison of viral advertising to television advertising. *Journal of Interactive Advertising, 6*. Retrieved from http://www.jiad.org/article78.html.

Powers, T., Advincula, D., Austin, M. S., & Graiko, S. (2013). Digital and social media in the purchase-decision process: A special report from the Advertising Research Foundation. *Journal of Advertising Research, 52*, 479-489. doi:10.2501/JAR-52-4-479-489.

Stelzner, M. (2014). *2014 social media marketing industry report.* Retrieved from http://www.socialmediaexaminer.com/social-media-marketing-industry-report-2014/.

Tucker, C. E. (2014). Social networks, personalized advertising, and privacy controls. *Journal of Marketing Research, 51*, 546-562. doi:10.1509/jmr.10.0355.

Weinberg, T. (2009). *The new community rules: Marketing on the social web.* Sebastopol, CA: O'Reilly Media Inc.

Witkemper, C., Choong Hoon, L., & Waldburger, A. (2012). Social media and sports marketing: Examining the motivations and constraints of Twitter users. *Sport Marketing Quarterly, 21*(3), 170-183.

NINE

Social Media Addiction

While previous chapters have discussed issues related to the dark side of social media—privacy and security, online deception and misinformation, narcissism, and the declining quality of interpersonal relationships—this chapter focuses on social media addiction. It discusses problems with defining social media addiction, its causes, and consequences. Although many newspaper articles have focused on the negative aspects of social media, very few research studies have been conducted in this area.

PROBLEMS WITH DEFINING SOCIAL MEDIA ADDICTION

While there are many positive uses of social media sites, overuse of social media is one of the negative components. Despite efforts to define social media addiction, a precise definition still does not exist. According to Griffiths (2000), an Internet user is considered addicted when the activity becomes the most important thing in the individual's life. It also includes withdrawal symptoms or negative feelings that accompany not being able to perform the online activity. Other symptoms include changes in mood and the need for more time or a new game to achieve a desired mood (Cash, Rae, Steel, & Winkler, 2012), unsuccessful efforts in trying to cut back Internet use, restlessness, and irritability (Beard, 2005).

There is no single official definition of social media addiction. Most studies have looked at Internet addiction only. Thus, different names have emerged to explain the same phenomenon: problematic Internet use (Davis, 2001), Internet dependence (Dowling & Quirk, 2009), compulsive Internet use, pathological Internet use (Caplan, 2002), and Internet addiction disorder. The most acceptable definition is Internet Addiction Disorder, defined by Byun et al. (2009) as excessive computer use that inter-feres with daily life. Although still not classified as a mental disorder, many researchers (e.g., Cash et al., 2012) have urged for it to be consid-ered for inclusion in the Diagnostic and Statistical Manual of Mental Disorders.

WHY ADDICTION TO SOCIAL MEDIA

Hormes, Kearns, and Alix Timko (2014) explained why someone could be addicted to a social network site. First, they have a number of characteris-tics that encourage users to recheck the sites frequently. For example, new material is constantly posted online, and when somebody comments on our posts, we get a mobile notification. This leads to rechecking the page multiple times. Another reason Hormes et al. (2014) proposed are difficulties with emotion regulation, poor impulse control, and difficul-ties engaging in goal-directed behaviors. For some users, social media are a way to escape reality, for others to cope with stress and depression. Overall, social media content is stimulating. This is the reason many have compared problematic Internet use to other types of problematic behav-ior, such as gambling (Young & Nabuco, 2011) or pornography (Cash et al., 2012).

There is also a biological explanation for addiction. According to Beard (2005), individuals who are more likely to get addicted are those with an insufficient amount of serotonin/dopamine. Serototin is a chemi-cal responsible for maintaining mood balance (medicinenet.com, 2014). Dopamine is a chemical that controls arousal, motivation, and reward. It is released in the brain as a result of rewarding experiences (e.g., food and sex) (Arias-Carrión & Pöppel, 2007). Playing social media games or just chatting with someone on Facebook can thus be rewarding, resulting in an increase in dopamine (Cash et al., 2012).

Tong, Vitak, and Larose (2010) also argued that many of the negative aspects of social media, such as addiction, stemmed from negative use by the users. The users already had some of the negative aspects that could be associated with social media. Therefore, it may not be social media that is bad, but those who use it. For example, a group of researchers have found (Aboujaoude, Koran, Gamel, Large, & Serpe, 2006) that one out of eight Americans exhibited at least one possible sign of problematic Internet use. When looking at the users of the 3D virtual world of Second Life, Gilbert, Murphy, and McNally (2011) found that approximately one-third of the participants met the criterion for Internet addiction. In addi-tion, their addiction was related to other compulsions in real life such as shopping, sex, gambling, drug, and alcohol addictions. This suggests that personality traits could predict addiction to social media. In fact, several studies (Cao & Su, 2006; Griffiths & Dancaster, 1995; Smahel, Brown, &

Blinka, 2012) found that low self-esteem, shyness, introversion, neuroticism, and a high degree of loneliness and depression might be what is causing individuals to spend too much time online. Another study (Hong, Huang, Lin, & Chiu, 2014) found a positive correlation between depression and addiction to Facebook. According to Hong et al., when the individual is unable to control one's own actions on Facebook, he or she experiences Facebook Addiction Disorder.

Research suggests that college women experience a significantly greater overall craving for Facebook than college men (Hormes et al., 2014). The explanation might be the fact that women already spend more time on Facebook (Sheldon, 2008) as they are more concerned about the main reason for using Facebook—to maintain interpersonal relationships. Other studies have suggested that people who score low in self-directedness score higher on online addiction, as they are not able to cope with problems in daily life (Kose, 2003; LaRose, Lin, & Eastin, 2003). Montag et al. (2011) suggested that providing addicts with a sense of achievement can boost their low self-esteem. In addition, people who are highly conscious are less likely to engage in problematic Internet use (Montag et al., 2011). Those people normally feel responsible for finishing a task and are highly productive at work.

An extensive literature review suggests that Internet addicts represent between 0.3 percent and 10.6 percent of the general population (Shaw & Black, 2008). The excessive use of new technologies is, however, most common among young people. In a study (Moeller, 2010) which included 12 campuses in 10 different countries, researchers found similar symptoms of social media addiction. When young adults (ages 17–23) were asked to give up social media for 24 hours, they experienced symptoms that were similar to a drug addiction. Eighty percent of students experienced mental and physical distress, panic, and confusion. Many reported feeling lonely, depressed, sad, and bored. According to research by Moreno et al. (2011), the mental health disorder most often associated with social network sites usage is depression.

Some researchers have suggested that there might be a chemical explanation for social media addiction. Looking at a chemical explanation for Facebook addiction, Horn (2012) reported that users experience psychophysiological responses when logging onto social network sites, similar to when users engaged in a creative activity. Simply logging onto a site such as Facebook can give people an adrenaline rush. "Liking" a status can feel rewarding and therefore increase the levels of dopamine. Grossman (2007) compares the addiction to heavy narcotics, like cocaine or crack. Other researchers (e.g., Alavi et al., 2012) found that behavioral addiction, such as Internet addiction, can be similar to substance addiction. For example, participants in a study conducted on twelve campuses reported "itching like a crackhead," feeling paralyzed, stressed, and anxious (Moeller, 2010). Another problem with social media is that they are free and easily available, compared to other substances that are expensive.

While substance addiction can be treated using total abstinence, due to the society in which we live, it is almost impossible for young people to give up social media all together. One of the suggestions is, therefore, to control the time spent on them (Griffiths, 2013). Hormes et al. (2014) suggested that the treatment techniques need to be similar to the ones for eating disorders, which include normalizing, rather than completely eliminating, problematic behavior. Other suggestions for Internet addiction have included using external stoppers or real events to force a patient to log off, using reminder cards, and entering support groups (Young, 1999). Edelstein (2014) also advises people to sign off from social media for a weekend, to implement rules, checking with purpose (e.g., seeing a relative's wedding photos), and buying an alarm clock.

There is not enough research to support whether any of these techniques would actually work with social media addicts.

NEGATIVE CONSEQUENCES OF SOCIAL MEDIA ADDICTION

Addiction to the Internet and social media can have a number of negative outcomes, including poor school performance (Tsitsika, Critselis, Louizou, Janikian, Freskou, Marangou, et al., 2011), poor workplace productivity, and a low quality of interpersonal relationships (Milani, Osualdella, & Di Blasio, 2009). Teenagers are constantly checking what others have posted on their Facebook or Twitter walls; the number of friends and followers, or the number of likes, have been more important than the quality of those friendships. Because nonverbal cues are absent, it is much easier to say "Happy Birthday" on Facebook than over the phone or face-to-face. However, a decline in the quality of our interpersonal relationships did not start with social media. In 1998, a group of researchers (Kraut, Patterson, Lundmark, Kiesler, Mukophadhyay, & Scherlis) discovered that people who spend more time online communicate less frequently with their family members. To this day we do not have many studies that explain how this quality has changed over the last decade, but each of us has been at a restaurant with friends when they suddenly become more obsessed with their smartphones than our conversation. According to the latest Pew Research Internet Project (2014) study, as of January 2014, 90 percent of Americans have a cell phone, and of those almost 60 percent have a smartphone.

Overall, it has been generally accepted that any kind of addiction is caused by a combination of biological, social, and psychological factors (Griffiths, 2005). When it comes to social skills, people who prefer virtual over face-to-face communication have inadequate self-presentational skills (Griffiths, 2013). They are addicted to social media, and especially social network sites, because they can present themselves in any way they want. In the short run, this leads to a higher life satisfaction; however, in the long run, it has adverse work and academic consequences.

REFERENCES

Aboujaoude, E., Koran, L. M., Gamel, N., Large, M., & Serpe, R. (2006). Potential markers for problematic Internet use: A telephone survey of 2,513 adults. *CNS Spectrums, 11*(10), 750-55.

Alavi, S., Ferdosi, M., Jannatifard, F., Eslami, M., Alaghemandan, H., & Setare, M. (2012). Behavioral addiction versus substance addiction: correspondence of psychiatric and psychological views. *International Journal of Preventative Medicine, 3*, 290-294.

Arias-Carrión, Ó., & Pöppel, E. (2007). Dopamine, learning, and reward-seeking behavior. *Acta Neurobiologiae Experimentalis, 67*(4), 481-488.

Beard, K. W. (2005). Internet addiction: A review of current assessment techniques and potential assessment questions. *CyberPsychology & Behavior, 8*, 7-14. doi:10.1089/cpb.2005.8.7.

Byun, S., Ruffini, C., Mills, J., Douglas, A., Niang, M., Stepchenkova, S., Lee, S., Loutfi, J., Lee, J., Atallah, M., & Blanton, M. (2009). Internet addiction: Metasynthesis of 1996–2006 quantitative research. *CyberPsychology & Behavior, 12*(2), 203-207. doi:10.1089/cpb.2008.0102.

Cash, H., Rae, C. D., Steel, A. H., & Winkler, A. (2012). Internet addiction: A brief summary of research and practice. *Current Psychiatry Reviews, 8*(4), 292-298. doi:10.2174/157340012803520513.

Cao, F., & Su, L. (2006). Internet addiction among Chinese adolescents: prevalence and psychological features. *Child: Care, Health & Development, 33*(3), 275–281.

Caplan, S. E. (2002). Problematic Internet use and psychosocial well-being: development of a theory-based cognitive-behavioral measurement instrument. *Computers in Human Behavior, 18*, 553–75. doi:10.1016/S0747-5632(02)00004-3.

Davis, R. A. (2001). A cognitive behavioral model of pathological internet use (PIU). *Computers in Human Behavior, 17*, 187-95. doi:10.1016/S0747-5632(00)00041-8.

Dowling, N. A, & Quirk, K. L. (2009). Screening for Internet dependence: Do the proposed diagnostic criteria differentiate normal from dependent Internet use? *CyberPsychology & Behavior, 12*, 21-7. doi:10.1089/cpb.2008.0162

Edelstein, J. (2014). Break free from social media. *Real Simple, 15*(1), 28.

Gilbert, R., Murphy, N., & McNally, T. (2011). Addiction to the 3-dimensional Internet: estimated prevalence and relationship to real world addictions. *Addiction Research & Theory, 19*, 380-390. doi:10.3109/16066359.2010.530714.

Griffiths, M. (2000). Does Internet and computer "addiction" exist? Some case study evidence. *CyberPsychology & Behavior, 3*, 211–218. doi:10.1089/109493100316067.

Griffiths, M. (2005). A "components" model of addiction within a biopsychosocial framework. *Journal of Substance Use, 10*, 191-197. doi:10.1080/14659890500114359.

Griffiths, M. (2013). Social networking addiction: Emerging themes and issues. *Addiction: Research & Therapy, 4*. doi:10.4172/2155-6105.1000e11. Retrieved from http://omicsonline.org/social-networking-addiction-emerging-themes-and-issues-2155-6105.1000e118.pdf.

Griffiths, M. D., & Dancaster, I. (1995). The effect of type A personality on physiological arousal while playing computer games. *Addictive Behaviors, 20*, 543–548. doi:10.1016/0306-4603(95)00001-S.

Grossman, L. (2007). The hyperconnected. *Time 169*(16), 54-56.

Hong, F., Huang, D., Lin, H., & Chiu, S. (2014). Analysis of the psychological traits, Facebook usage, and Facebook addiction model of Taiwanese university students. *Telematics and Informatics, 31,* 597-606. doi:10.1016/j.tele.2014.01.001.

Hormes, J. M., Kearns, B., & Alix Timko, C. (2014). Craving Facebook? Behavioral addiction to online social networking and its association with emotion regulation deficits. *Addiction, 109,* 2079-2088. doi:10.1111/add.12713.

Horn, L. (2012). Study finds chemical reason behind Facebook 'addiction.' *PC Magazine,* 1.

Kose, S. (2003). Psychobiological model of temperament and character. *Yeni Symposium, 41,* 86-97.

Kraut, R., Patterson, M., Lundmark, V., Kiesler, S., Mukopadhyay, T., & Scherlis, W. (1998). Internet paradox: A social technology that reduces social involvement and psychological well-being? *American Psychologist, 53,* 1017-1031. doi:10.1037/0003-066X.53.9.1017.

LaRose, R., Lin, C. A., & Eastin, M. (2003). Unregulated Internet usage: Addiction, habit, or deficient self-regulation? *Media Psychology, 5,* 225-253. doi:10.1207/S1532785XMEP0503_01.

Medicinenet.com (2014). *Definition of serotonin.* Retrieved from http://www.medicinenet.com/script/main/art.asp?articlekey=5468.

Milani, L., Osualdella, D., & Di Blasio, P. (2009). Quality of interpersonal relationships and problematic Internet use in adolescence. *CyberPsychology & Behavior, 12*(6), 681-684. doi:10.1089/cpb.2009.0071.

Moeller, S. (2010). *The world unplugged.* Retrieved from http://theworldunplugged.wordpress.com/.

Montag, C., Flierl, M., Markett, S., Walter, N., Jurkiewicz, M., & Reuter, M. (2011). Internet addiction and personality in first-person-shooter video gamers. *Journal of Media Psychology, 23,* 163-173.doi:10.1027/1864-1105/a000049.

Moreno, M., Jelenchick, L., Egan, K., Cox, E., Young, H., Gannon, K., & Becker, T. (2011). Feeling bad on Facebook: Depression disclosures by college students on a social networking site. *Depression and Anxiety, 28*(6), 447-455. doi:10.1002/da.20805.

Pew Research Internet Project (2014). *Mobile technology fact sheet.* Retrieved from http://www.pewinternet.org/fact-sheets/mobile-technology-fact-sheet/.

Shaw, M., & Black, D. W. (2008). Internet addiction: Definition, assessment, epidemiology and clinical management. *CNS Drugs, 22,* 353-365.

Sheldon, P. (2008). Student favorite: Facebook & motives for its use. *Southwestern Mass Communication Journal, 23,* 39-55.

Smahel, D., Brown, B. B., and Blinka, L. (2012). Associations between online friendship and Internet addiction among adolescents and emerging adults. *Developmental Psychology, 48,* 381-388. doi:10.1037/a0027025.

Tong, S., Vitak, J., & LaRose, R. (2010). Truly problematic or merely habitual? An integrated model of the negative consequences of social networking. *Conference Papers—International Communication Association.*

Tsitsika, A., Critselis, E., Louizou, A., Janikian, M., Freskou, A., Marangou, E., et al. (2011). Determinants of Internet addiction among adolescents: A case-control study. *The Scientific World Journal, 11,* 866-874. doi:10.1100/tsw.2011.85.

Young, K. S. (1999). Internet addiction: Symptoms, evaluation, and treatment. *Innovations in clinical practice.* Retrieved from http://www.netaddiction.com/articles/symptoms.pdf.

Young, K. S, & Nabuco, de Abreu C. (2011). *Internet addiction: A handbook and guide to evaluation and treatment.* New Jersey: John Wiley & Sons Inc.

Appendix

Brief History of Social Media

The history of social media started with the first virtual community created in 1978, when computer scientists Murray Turoff and S. Roxanne Hiltz established the Electronic Information Exchange System (EIES) at the New Jersey Institute of Technology (Acar, 2008). EIES was seen as one of the first collective intelligence projects. EIES allowed users to e-mail each other, see a bulletin board, and utilize the list serve (Hiltz & Turoff, 1978; 1993; Wasserman & Faust, 1994). The system was also used to deliver courses, conduct conferencing sessions, and facilitate research. Development of EIES was funded by the National Science Foundation to further explore the potential for computer conferencing. EIES had more than 2,000 subscribers from companies such as Exxon and IBM, government agencies, and universities around the United States ("IRC History," 2000). The same year that EIES was completed, the "bulletin board system" was invented in 1978. The first bulletin boards were text-based and allowed two or more computers to communicate using modems and telephone lines. They remained the primary kind of online community until the early 1990s, before the World Wide Web arrived ("The BBC Corner," 2009). In 1989, Tim Berners-Lee created the World Wide Web, and soon the blogging began.

The very first blog was introduced in 1994 by Justin Hall, a student at Swarthmore College, who started his personal web diary, *Justin's Links from the Underground*, at www.links.net. Hall was a student intern at San Francisco-based *Wired* magazine at that time (Harmanci, 2005). In 1997, Jorn Barger of the weblog *Robot Wisdom* (robotwisdom.com) coined the term "weblog," meaning logging the Web. Later, Peter Merholz broke the word weblog into the phrase "we blog," thus shortening "weblog" to "blog." Evan Williams from Pyra Labs used the term "blog" as both a noun and verb, and devised a new term "blogger" ("Origins of Blog," 2008).

In 1998–1999, the most popular blog platforms emerged. Open Diary launched in 1998. LiveJournal and Blogger were created in 1999. In 2000, Andrew Sullivan launched the Daily Dish, one of the very first political blogs. A number of political blogs emerged in 2001. Several people became famous because of blogs. In 2002, Heather Armstrong was fired for writing about people at her job on her personal blog, dooce.com. The term "dooced" then emerged, meaning "to lose one's job because of one's website" (urbandictionary.com). Blogs were the most popular type of social media around 2003–2004, before the emergence of social network sites.

The first online social network was created in 1997, and it was called SixDegrees.com (boyd & Ellison, 2007). The creator, Andrew Weinreich, got an idea that came from Milgram's famous small-world study that any one person is connected to any other person through six or fewer relationships. Another social network was created in 2001. Adrian Scott founded a website called Ryze.com. Ryze was designed to link business professionals, an idea similar to LinkedIn. The name of the social network came from the words "rise up," "because it's about people helping each other 'rise up' through quality networking." In 2002, Canadian computer programmer Jonathan Abrams launched Friendster.com. Friendster was designed to help friends-of-friends meet and it was the first network to reach one million members. The site lost popularity after the introduction of MySpace and Facebook and was later redesigned as a local gaming site (boyd & Ellison, 2007; "Friendster Back," 2012). In August 2003, Chris deWolfe and Tom Anderson created Myspace.com (Lapinski, 2006). MySpace was a pop music hub that helped many musicians launch their careers. From 2005 until early 2008, MySpace was the most visited site in the world, surpassing Google in June 2006 (Cashmore, 2006). In April 2008, Facebook surpassed MySpace in the number of unique visitors, and since then it has declined steadily (Albanesius, 2009). The idea of selfies, however, originated on MySpace. A number of popular social network sites were created in 2003 and 2004. LinkedIn (LinkedIn® professional networking services), a business-oriented social network site, was established in 2003 in Mountain View, California. LinkedIn's founders are Reid Hoffman, Allen Blue, Konstantin Guericke, Eric Ly, and Jean-Luc Vaillant. In 2004, Facebook was created as the main competitor to MySpace. Mark Zuckerberg created facebook.com to replace the paper facebook, or a class directory, that was given to freshmen as part of their introduction to a new school (Carlson, 2012). The website's membership was initially limited to Harvard students, but was expanded to other colleges in the Boston area and the Ivy League. It later expanded further to include any university student, then high school students, and finally, anyone aged 13 and over. In 2006, Jack Dorsey, Noah Glass, Biz Stone, and Evan Williams created Twitter, another popular social network site. The idea of Twitter is to send and receive short messages (no more than 140 characters). In 2010, Instagram was created by Kevin Systrom and Mike Krieger. Pinterest, another popular image-sharing social networking site, was also created in 2010 (Mull & Lee, 2014). In 2012, Google launched Google+.

Another form of social media are wikis. The word "wiki" is a Hawaiian term for "fast." Wikis are collaborative projects, seen as a special form of social media application, that enable the joint and simultaneous creation of knowledge-related content by many end users (Kaplan & Haenlein, 2014). Wikis are the most democratic form of social media because they allow anyone to add, delete, or revise content on a webpage by using a simple web browser (Kaplan & Haenlein, 2014). The most popular wiki today is Wikipedia. Wikipedia is a free-access, multilingual online encyclopedia, founded by Jimmy Wales and Larry Sanger in 2001 (Sidener, 2004). Wikipedia changed the idea of how knowledge is stored and accessed. Unlike traditional media where only experts could publish entries, Wikipedia allows any reader to be an editor.

YouTube, a video-sharing site, was created in 2005 by three PayPal employees: Steve Chen, Chad Hurley, and Jawed Karim. The site allows users to upload their own videos, as well as watch the videos of other users. YouTube has been used by different audiences including private individuals, companies who advertise on the site, as well as politicians and government. YouTube played an important role in the 2010 Arab Spring movement and some people have become popular because of their appearance on YouTube. One of those people is Susan Boyle, a Scottish singer who became famous after appearing on the *Britain's Got Talent* show.

REFERENCES

Acar, A. (2008). Antecedents and consequences of online social networking behavior: The case of Facebook. *Journal of Website Promotion, 3*, 62-83. doi:10.1080/15533610802052654.

Albanesius, C. (2009, June 16). *More Americans go to Facebook than MySpace.* Retrieved from http://www.pcmag.com/article2/0,2817,2348822,00.asp.

"The BBC Corner—A Brief History of BBS Systems" (2009). Retrieved from http://www.bbscorner.com/usersinfo/bbshistory.htm.

boyd, d. m., and Ellison, N. B. (2007). Social network sites: Definition, history, and scholarship. *Journal of Computer-Mediated Communication, 13*(1), article 11. Retrieved from http://jcmc.indiana.edu/vol13/issue1/Boyd.ellison.html.

Carlson, N. (2012, May 1). Inside Pinterest: An overnight success four years in the making. *Business Insider.* Retrieved from http://www.businessinsider.com/inside-pinterest-an-overnight-success-four-years-in-the-making-2012-4.

Cashmore, P. (2006, July 11). *MySpace, America's number one.* Retrieved from http://mashable.com/2006/07/11/myspace-americas-number-one/.

"Friendster back with social network" (2012). *Social media today.* Retrieved from http://socialmediatoday.com/mohammed-anzil/1113891/friendster-back-social-network.

Harmanci, R. (2005, February 20). Time to get a life—pioneer blogger Justin Hall bows out at 31. *San Francisco Chronicle.* Retrieved from http://www.sfgate.com/news/article/Time-to-get-a-life-pioneer-blogger-Justin-Hall-2697359.php.

Hiltz, S. R., and Turoff, M. (1978). *The network nation: Human communication via computer.* Reading, MA: Addison-Wesley.

Hiltz, S. R.,and Turoff, M. (1993). *The network nation: Human communication via computer, revised edition.* Cambridge, MA: MIT Press.

"IRC history—Electronic Information Exchange System" (2000). Retrieved from http://www.livinginternet.com/r/ri_eies.htm.

Kaplan, A., and Haenlein, M. (2014). Collaborative projects (social media application): About Wikipedia, the free encyclopedia. *Business Horizons, 57*(5), 617-626. doi:10.1016/j.bushor.2014.05.004.

Lapinski, T. (2006). MySpace: The business of spam 2.0. ValleyWag. Retrieved from http://valleywag.com/tech/myspace/myspace-the-business-of-spam-20-exhaustive -edition-199924.php.

Mull, I. R., and Lee, S. (2014). "PIN" pointing the motivational dimensions behind Pinterest. *Computers in Human Behavior, 33,* 192-200. doi:10.1016/j.chb.2014.01.011.

Origins of "Blog" and "Blogger." American Dialect Society Mailing List (2008, April 20).

Sidener, J. (2004, December 6). *Everyone's encyclopedia.* Retrieved from http://www.utsandiego.com/uniontrib/20041206/news_mz1b6encyclo.html.

Wasserman, S., and Faust, K. (1994). *Social network analysis: Methods and applications.* Cambridge, UK: Cambridge University Press.

Index

About the Author

Dr. Pavica Sheldon is an assistant professor in the Department of Communication Arts at University of Alabama in Huntsville. She holds a BA in Journalism from the University of Zagreb, an MMC, and a PhD in Communication Studies from Louisiana State University (2010). She is an author of more than a dozen peer-reviewed articles on the uses and effects of social media, primarily Facebook. Her hobbies include dancing Zumba, exercising, and photography.